Just Write It!

Just Write It!

How to develop top-class university writing skills

Greta Solomon

Open University Press

Open University Press
McGraw-Hill Education
McGraw-Hill House
Shoppenhangers Road
Maidenhead
Berkshire
England
SL6 2QL

email: enquiries@openup.co.uk
world wide web: www.openup.co.uk

and Two Penn Plaza, New York, NY 10121–2289, USA

First published 2013

A catalogue record of this book is available from the British Library

ISBN-13: 978–0–33–524599–4 (pb)
ISBN-10: 0–33–524599–4 (pb)
eISBN: 978–0–33–524600–7

Library of Congress Cataloging-in-Publication Data
CIP data applied for

Typesetting and e-book compilations by
RefineCatch Limited, Bungay, Suffolk
Printed and bound by CPI Group (UK) Ltd, Croydon, CR0 4YY

Praise for this book

"The biggest fear and indeed stumbling block for some students is their writing skills, yet the ability to articulate yourself in a written format is vital for success. Writing is a skill that develops over time with practice. Indeed, if I were learning to ride a motorbike, I would seek assistance along the way and may also occasionally fall over and scrape my knees, yet often students do not apply this same mentality when it comes to developing their writing skills. Just Write it! is a reader-friendly, step by step book, which demystifies academic writing and breaks the process down in bite-sized chunks. It offers great practical advice and assistance in simple stages, which guide the reader to developing their writing skills."

Vanessa Heaslip, Senior Lecturer in Adult Nursing, Bournemouth University, UK

"This is a well-designed book to support undergraduates through their university journey. It is user-friendly with its clear, easy to follow structure. This book is a great support mechanism to help undergraduates to achieve. I highly recommend this text - it is an essential resource for undergraduates!"

Emma Jackson, University of Worcester, UK

Contents

Preface: A letter to the reader

Have you ever instinctively known what to do at a given moment? Or experienced a chance meeting or chain of events that seemed to have its own life force? This is how it felt when I started to get inklings that what I should really do is teach. So, in 2006 I heeded my calling. Until then, I had been a writer, journalist and public relations (PR) practitioner. I had spent several years writing for women's magazines and PR clients. But something – fate, the universe or a plain old hunch – told me that what I really needed to do was inspire other people to find their own voices.

I signed up with a tutoring agency and students started to trickle in. Then the word started to go round my area. 'Did you know there's this tutor who helps people improve by two grades?' the parents of my students would say to each other. Before long, I was inundated for requests for tuition and had a long waiting list for my services.

I have worked with hundreds of students aged 6 to 60. I have coached them to pass their SATs, 11+ and 13+ entrance exams, GCSEs, A-levels and degrees. I helped them to write personal statements and CVs and shared interview tips and techniques. Simon, whose teacher had threatened to relegate him to the bottom set in GCSE English if his grades didn't improve, suddenly stunned the faculty by scoring straight As. Melanie won a full scholarship to a coveted grammar school. And special needs student Raj went from a grade F to a grade C in GCSE English, finding confidence in his self-expression abilities along the way.

With all these achievements under my belt, I started focusing almost exclusively on university students, of all disciplines, and the success stories kept rolling in. Philosophy and French graduate Paulina channelled her new-found interest in words into a journalism career. Meanwhile, mature Nursing student Terence was able to verbalize intellectually but every time he came to write, he would freeze. Yet, he was able to build the confidence to pass all his assignments when many people at his university failed.

But perhaps the biggest success was the method I created, which is what I will share with you in this book. I found that as soon as my students increased their creativity and levels of self-expression, they were able to think more freely and confidently and were able to successfully implement writing skills techniques that transformed all their written work.

So, this book is inspired by my students. The exercises are the result of the many hours we spent working together, as I created and tested new writing skills methods on them. The result is that this book is an incredibly practical programme and you will learn simply by completing the exercises.

Now, teaching writing has taken me all over the world to places such as Norway, Ethiopia and Holland where I have delivered corporate writing skills workshops for various organizations. I have also taught senior executives at a world-leading charity how to write stories that touch people's hearts and encourage donors to give money that can save children's lives. I have seen the power of words and the joy on my students' faces when something suddenly clicks and they realize that they can write freely and expressively. The confidence that it promotes in their studies, lives, work and well-being is priceless.

And so, dear reader, my aim in this book is for you to feel the same levels of confidence and self-expression. I hope that somewhere between deadlines, responsibilities and the pressures of taking a degree you can carve out a little space to practise your writing. I hope that you experience the delight of being able to communicate freely, clearly and concisely. But most of all, I hope that when you hear the siren call of serendipity you'll be right there, ready and waiting to take action.

Acknowledgements

This book is dedicated to my late mother, Joy Solomon. She inspired in me a love of words and a love of writing and for that I will always be grateful.

Special thanks go to my husband Krister Kristiansen for his unwavering love and support.

Thank you to Katherine Hartle, Verity Holliday, Shona Mullen, Abbie Jones and the rest of the team at McGraw-Hill.

Finally, thank you to all my students who have supported the development of this book.

Introduction

You've made it! After months of revision, tackling panic-inducing exam questions and a nail-biting wait for your results – you're finally at university. Now, what? Well, with the celebrations firmly over you're left with a far more sobering reality.

For a start, you're expected to read and digest copious amounts of complex information. You're then expected to use that information independently to come up with your own intellectual stance. And the stakes are high. Depending on where you're studying, Sir Isaac Newton, Oscar Wilde or Edward de Bono could have walked the halls before you.

But that's not all. The university landscape is almost unrecognizable from school classrooms. Words such as 'discourse' and 'deontology' are casually bandied about. You're expected to step up and become a confident, *academic* writer. In fact, a study by researcher Lisa Ganobcsik-Williams (2004) found that 98 per cent of university tutors expect your writing to improve significantly throughout your course. But having written all your life, it can seem like all the rules have changed and that you have no idea how to write a degree standard essay, let alone emulate the great academics. It's enough to make even the most confident student break out in a cold sweat.

What is academic writing?

Contrary to popular belief, academic writing doesn't have to be pompous and hard to decipher with long, winding sentences that only lead to fear and trepidation. Granted, you may feel that some of your textbooks are written in the academic equivalent of hieroglyphics. But that doesn't mean that you have to emulate that style.

Put simply, academic writing uses other people's work to evaluate, compare and contrast viewpoints, and then it discusses them at length. The subject matter may be different, but we all do the same with our friends when discussing music, films or sport. However, most students get tripped up by the conventional way in which this is done. Academic style is cautious and neutral. For instance, instead of writing: 'I think', the convention is to write: 'It seems that' (or some other cautious variation).

However, the trouble is that most students haven't been taught to write in the first place. So faced with what seems like a whole new way of writing, they rely too much on quotes, definitions and regurgitating what other academics have said.

If you've picked up this book, it's likely that you wish you could write in an easier, quicker and more effective way. Well, the good news is that no matter your current level of ability you can learn simple techniques that will transform your writing. You don't have to rely on writing crutches and props. Whether you're a first, second or final year student you can benefit from this book.

Working through this book is like having your very own writing coach guiding you and coaxing out of you clear, crisp, creative and effective pieces of writing. The interactive exercises, activities, quizzes and tasks each build on a fundamental principle of writing.

Just Write It! is a set system to unlock your creativity and bring it back to life. Think of it as a word workout where you are flexing your writing muscles in a skilled, controlled way. The more creative you are as a writer, the more you will be up to the academic demands of your course.

It must be noted here that this book uses a very informal style, which includes contractions such as 'isn't' and 'didn't'. This is to make the book easy to read and accessible. But in all your academic work you should write out the words in full. This means that 'isn't' becomes 'is not' and 'didn't' becomes 'did not'. Once you've mastered excellent writing skills, you're free to use creative licence outside and beyond university to write in this more informal way.

The nuts and bolts of the programme

To get the most out of this book, it's best to follow it in order, which may take three months or up to a year. The only exception is Part IV. Some of the exercises there can be completed in order, but others are most useful if you actually have an essay or dissertation to write, or an exam to prepare for. Overall, the most important thing is that you use the 'little and often' approach when it comes to this programme.

The book is divided into five sections. The first lays the foundation for good writing. You'll figure out exactly what's holding you back from your writing best and then set a series of goals. Then you'll go back to basics with reading and vocabulary exercises.

In the second part of the book, you'll learn how to access your seven senses and use objects to kick-start your creativity. You'll also learn techniques for creating metaphors, plus practical ways of putting your new-found creative skills to good use.

Part III is the thinking phase, where you'll learn to recognize the differences between right and left brain thinking and how to integrate the two. You'll identify your thinking type and learn techniques for planning, generating ideas and persuading.

Part IV is the practical application of everything you have learnt. You'll learn, step by step, how to apply your new knowledge to essays (both coursework and exam), dissertations, articles and reports. And you'll learn fresh ways to approach these types of written work. We'll also look at writing effective personal statements, CVs and cover letters. And you'll learn how to transform academic writing into writing that thrives in the business world.

Finally, in the finishing touches section, there is an extensive checklist where you can mark off the techniques you have learnt and ensure that you are using them in your essays and other work. This checklist is a document you can visit again and again.

If you don't have the luxury of several months and need a quick fix, you can dip in and out of any of the chapters and exercises. But you'll see the biggest and most long-lasting change if you follow the programme as it's laid out. This is because each stage builds upon the last.

Graduation and beyond

Just Write It! isn't a magic wand, but if you diligently apply the exercises, you will gain essential writing skills that will last a lifetime. This book is about writing with a practical purpose. It aims to give you the skills to write effectively and creatively on all subjects and to become a fluent, passionate communicator. This is essential in order to respond to the demands of our fast-moving society, which is constantly changing and evolving. Empower yourself by assuming personal responsibility for the quality of your writing skills. Adopting an empowered attitude will take you far – not to mention helping you get the best university grades possible!

Part I

Laying the foundations

Chapter 1

Have you got the write stuff?

Welcome to *Just Write It!* You might be a little surprised that you're not actually going to do any writing composition in this chapter. Instead you're going to examine your thoughts, feelings and beliefs about writing, which will help pave the way to becoming a whole-brain writer.

This chapter is crucial because it's part of the foundation for the work ahead. So, whatever you do, don't skip it. The more time you spend on these quizzes and exercises, the better results you'll see later.

So, let's begin.

Read the statements below and tick all that apply to you. Don't worry – there are no right or wrong answers.

Writing is . . .

Worse than a nightmare ❑

Really hard work ❑

A struggle to get my thoughts on paper ❑

A chore that I hate doing ❑

A fun way to express my thoughts and feelings ❑

A natural thing I do all the time ❑

Sometimes challenging, but really satisfying	❑
A complete mystery to me	❑
OK, except for all that spelling and grammar	❑
Something with right and wrong answers	❑
A talent you are born with	❑
Just another part of university that I can take or leave	❑

How did you do? Were you really honest? Did some of your answers surprise you?

Whether you love writing, hate writing or feel nothing towards it, you need to be actively aware of what you're thinking.

Tick which writing category you belong in

Like	❑
Love	❑
Hate	❑
Indifference	❑

Next, let's delve a little deeper.

What (if anything) do you like about writing and why?

____

____

____

What (if anything) do you hate about writing and why?

If you ticked the 'indifference' category, explain why. For example, what does writing mean to you?

What writing tasks do you find the easiest?

What writing tasks are the hardest for you?

The chances are good that you like the tasks you find easy. The aim of this book is to make the process of writing a lot easier and, in turn, more enjoyable.

Cultivating a writing mind

You've faced up to how you really think and feel about writing. Now it's time to change some of your thinking. This is crucial as your thoughts and feelings, in large part, create your reality. Much of what you may believe about writing are actually myths – ideas which simply aren't true.

Let's take the example of Brussels sprouts. If you think that sprouts are tasty, then you will enjoy eating them. If you think they're the worst vegetable ever, again, that's your reality. The truth is, Brussels sprouts are not inherently yummy or yucky – it's all a matter of perspective. But, if you hate them, you can train your mind to like them and actually even enjoy them. It's the same with your writing.

Psychologist Seymour Epstein has spent his career looking at people's mindsets. He devised the Constructive Thinking Inventory (Epstein 1998), and stated that constructive thinking is the key to managing your emotions, developing emotional intelligence (which we'll look at in Chapter 2) and dealing with stress.

Here are some examples of constructive thinking versus destructive thinking:

Table 1.1 Examples of constructive versus destructive thinking

Destructive thinking	*Constructive thinking*
To be good at writing I have to know everything about spelling and grammar.	I can learn practical techniques as I go along. This book is a journey, where step by step I'll learn what I need to learn.
People who are good at writing are just smarter than everyone else.	Writing is something that I can learn. The more I do targeted, focused practice, using the exercises in the book, the better I'll get. Of course, some writers are very smart but it doesn't mean that good writers are a breed apart from everyone else.
People who are good at writing find that words just flow to them.	Writing takes concentration and effort – good writers may make it look easy but they are thinking hard and finding the best words to put on the page. Besides, anything worth doing takes time to master.

People who are good at writing are inspired – everything comes naturally to them.	My inspiration will come and go, but as long as I start somewhere I can grow my ideas from there. I need to do independent work most days so I can't wait to be inspired. I've got to be able to sit down and do it no matter how I feel.
Writing is agony and torture.	Everything is what I make it. I choose to see writing as a challenge rather than a source of pain. Although writing can sometimes feel like a chore, once I get into it, I can enjoy it.
Writing should be fun and easy all the time. If it's not, I must be doing it incorrectly.	Sometimes writing will be fun and easy, and other times it will be difficult and demanding. I need to celebrate the successes I have and remember that being able to write well will put me ahead of other people in both university and life.
I should be smart enough to instantly write like a university lecturer and cope with difficult essays.	Everything worth having takes time to learn. I can learn the differences between A-level and university essays and apply new techniques step by step.
To succeed at university I have to have the intelligence of a Nobel Prize winner.	I can learn thinking techniques that give my IQ a workout – I don't have to be perfect to be a success.

Recognizing your writing behaviours

So, we've looked at which thoughts about writing are helpful, and which are not so helpful. Now, see if you recognize yourself in any of the characters below. Then think about whether your behaviour helps you to achieve your goals. We'll look in more detail at goal setting in Chapter 2. But for now, just think about whether your behaviour around writing and university work helps you to get what you want: whether it's good grades, plenty of time to play football or a congratulatory gift to yourself for being so smart!

Quiz: What type of writer are you?

Over the next week monitor all your actions around your writing. Or, if you don't think that's going to work, ask a friend or study partner to keep an eye on what you actually do when you've got a pen, pencil or keyboard in your hands.

Writing types

Perfectionist Petra

Your attitude is that your writing is either perfect or worthless. You spend ages on one assignment or piece of work and feel that everything you do is never quite good enough. Ironically, your work has plenty of crossings out because you always want your writing to be exact and precise. Highly conscientious, you are a hard worker who gets good marks.

Fretful Fred

You hate seeing your lecturer's red pen across your work. So you play it safe and don't take too many writing risks. This means you tend to follow set patterns in your work and don't like to try out new techniques or ideas.

Could Do Better Betty

You simply never put 100 per cent into anything. You know that you have huge potential, but instead prefer to do just enough to get by. Your friends and lecturers don't think you're particularly smart, but you occasionally pull out the stops and get excellent marks, before going back to your easy life. The downside is that gaps are forming in your knowledge and you are finding it more difficult to maintain your grades.

Fun-seeking Fehmina

You prefer not to think too much and would much rather be active and outdoors than cooped up over a textbook and a pad of paper. Having fun is the most important thing and writing just doesn't compete with other activities.

Slapdash Simon

You whittle off work at an amazing speed but your work is littered with silly errors that would have been spotted with a little more care and attention. You also leap in and start working before even formulating a plan.

Last-minute Lorraine

You often hand work in late because you simply haven't given yourself enough time to complete it. With every piece of work it's as though you're competing in a 100m race because you avoid doing most written work until the very last minute.

One-Trick Oliver

You quite like writing certain things – your music blog, for instance. But when it comes to something you find challenging, you freeze up. Sometimes, you can get going but find it hard to finish. Other times, you feel you just don't have the skills to get a university essay done.

Using affirmations to change your mind and behaviours

Whether you identify with some of the types, all of them, or none at all – questioning your writing behaviour is the first step to success. Once you've identified your negative thoughts and attitudes about writing you can use affirmations to help change them.

Often used by psychologists and life coaches, affirmations are short statements of positive intent that state in the present what you would like to 'do', 'have' or 'be' in life. Although it may seem a little simple, creating affirmations and repeating them is incredibly powerful. This is because much of our behaviour is ruled by our subconscious minds – the part of our brains that is automatic. The subconscious rules our breathing, the nervous system and other functions that don't need conscious thought.

When we're actively thinking about something, it is our conscious mind at play. For instance, if you're learning to play tennis, you have to make a real effort to think about your technique and the strokes you're making. But once you've mastered that backhand or volley, it becomes automatic and you no longer think about it.

Our behaviours and thoughts operate in much the same way. If, way back at first school, you started thinking that writing was really hard, and quite frankly a bit of a nightmare, the chances are good that every time you wrote you activated that thought. Soon after, just like learning the backhand, that thought became automatic and you didn't even really notice it. Then it turned into behaviours, so that every time you wrote, it actually was a hard slog.

Writing may still be hard and a nightmare but you don't have to think that it is. You can train your mind to think more positively and in turn that will make the experience a lot more enjoyable, which will in turn make it much easier to create change.

Creating affirmations

Now's the time to create some affirmations for your writing – make sure you create at least three and up to 10, if necessary. Affirmations work best when you say them in the present tense as though they are already happening. Start each one with 'I am', 'I think', 'I can' or 'Writing is.' For example, you might say, 'I am writing in an easy, fluent way' or, 'I can find great ideas for essays everywhere.'

But don't just pull these affirmations out of the sky. Go back to your original statements (including what you found hard about writing and everything we've done in this chapter so far) and see where your danger spots were. Then, turn your thoughts on their head. So, if at the start of this chapter you thought that writing was a chore that you hated doing, your affirmation might be, 'Writing is something that I approach with all my energy' or, 'Writing is something I enjoy.'

If you identified with Slapdash Simon in the writing types, you might say, 'I am taking time to write more slowly, with more care.'

On the flip side, if you have a pretty positive attitude to writing, just create a couple of statements that back up your current attitude.

Affirmation sheet

1 ____

____

2 ____

____

3 ____

____

4 ____

____

5 ____

____

6 ____

____

7 ____

____

8 ____

____

9 ____

____

10 ____

____

Why are affirmations so important?

These affirmations will help to trick your brain into solving your writing problems, while you focus on other things. We've got a lot of work to do in the coming chapters. We have to make sure that the terrain is as smooth as possible, so that the going doesn't get too tough.

For this reason, it's important to remedy your thoughts before you put pen to paper for a single writing exercise. Preparation can be the single biggest factor in whether you succeed or fail. If you're well prepared you're better at navigating obstacles as they come your way.

What next?

Now that you've written your affirmations, your task is to pick the most important ones and read these every morning and evening out loud for the next 30 days. If reading them aloud is a little dull, you can sing them, chant them or spell them out with your alphabet spaghetti at dinner time. Just say them somehow until you actually start to believe them.

Research by Dr Maxwell Maltz (1960) found that it takes 21 days to form a habit. But it can actually take up to 245 days to really ingrain this new habit (Lally *et al.* 2010). Of course, you're free to repeat your affirmations for much longer than 30 days. But a 30-day time frame is a realistic way to get started. After this period you can work with different affirmations or simply reap the rewards of the affirmations you've already worked with.

Now, you may find that every time you say an affirmation, such as 'I can write easily and well', another part of you answers back with, 'No, you can't!'

Don't worry about this, just keep going with your positive thoughts and soon the negative ones will be drowned out.

Dealing with corrections and criticisms

It can also be hard to keep thinking positively about your writing when your lecturers give back your work, smeared with red marks, highlighting all the things you did wrong. It also doesn't help if you put all your energy into something and still get the same old marks as when you didn't try.

Learning to apply the right tools helps get past this last problem. The first problem is all about mind control. So, try not to think constantly about what mark you're going to get; just make the writing the best you can. Think of your grades as being fluid and know that with hard work, learning and application of new skills you can change your grades. Grades are not set in stone. A bad grade today does not mean a bad grade tomorrow and a good grade today does not guarantee a good grade tomorrow.

Understanding whole-brain writing

The good news is that you have begun to understand your thoughts and behaviour as a writer. Now, you need to take the first steps into understanding yourself as a whole-brain writer. And to do this, first we have to look at neuroscience. If the mere mention of science brings you out in a cold sweat, relax. This is brain science with a purpose. It's going to make you into a happier, more confident writer. It helps to understand the principles behind the methods in this book, so you can not only master them but perhaps also share them with others.

Although humans only have one brain, studies have shown that the brain is split into right and left hemispheres. These opposite areas, or spheres, communicate to each other through a thick band that contains millions of nerve fibres called the corpus callosum.

Now, here's the interesting part. Neuroscientists Roger Sperry and Michael Gazzaniga studied patients whose corpus callosum had been cut (Gazzaniaga 2005). Although these patients with 'split brains' seemed perfectly normal at first, it soon emerged that the right and left hemispheres of the brain were responsible for different functions. They found that the right side of the brain could not process language (or writing). That was the domain of the left side. The left hand side of the brain was responsible for language, calculations, maths, detail, analysis and logical abilities. In contrast, the right was found to be non-verbal and primarily responsible for spatial abilities, face recognition, pattern recognition, visual imagery and music appreciation. Put simply, the right side of the brain is involved in the creative, intuitive aspects whereas the left side is more logical.

A nation of left-brain writers

Despite writing being a primarily left-brain activity, it's important to remember that you actually use your whole brain when you do any task. The trouble is that right-brain activities get sidelined in schools, so people become over-reliant on the left brain. School develops our logical abilities, teaching us to analyse, add up and deduce one thing from another. This is great, except that the more left-brained we become, the less we're able to write freely and easily. The left logical brain wants to edit, cross things out and have everything in a neat linear fashion. And most of the time, writing just isn't like that. The left brain may control our ability to write. But the right brain needs to get involved, otherwise we can feel frustrated, blocked and simply unable to get the words onto the page.

Quiz: are you more right-brained or left-brained?

This quiz is based on the Myers-Briggs Type Indicator, which is a questionnaire that measures how people perceive the world and make decisions (MBTI Basics 2012). The Indicator results in 16 discrete personality types. But we're just using some of the principles to find out whether you are more right-brained or left-brained. Finding out your preference can help you to know exactly what you need to work on with your writing.

Tick whether you agree or disagree with the following statements:

Category 1: facts versus ideas

Left-brain statements	**Agree**	**Disagree**
I like to work with facts and figures		
I don't like to accept things without proof		
I pay close attention to detail in my university work		
I like things to be routine and predictable		
Right-brain statements		
I'm a dreamer and want life to be like my ideals		
I am very resourceful and creative when solving problems		
I think about the future a lot and am open to many possibilities		
I love it when the rules constantly change		

Category 2: thoughts versus feelings

Left-brain statements	**Agree**	**Disagree**
I'm good at planning and organizing		
I like to put things into categories		
I think a lot about concrete things rather than ideas		
In writing, I tend to put 'I think . . .'		
Right-brain statements		
In teamwork, I think of others before making decisions		
I'm good at imagining how people feel		
I consult how I feel before I make decisions		
In writing, I tend to put 'I feel . . .'		

Category 3: structured versus flexible

Left-brain statements	**Agree**	**Disagree**
I don't like leaving work half-finished		
I'm good at sticking to a schedule		
I choose the safe approach and don't take risks		
I can make decisions easily and stick to them		
Right-brain statements		
I often leave work half-finished		
I'm good at doing lots of things at once		
I'm curious about people, situations and ideas		
I find it hard to choose anything!		

What does it mean?

It's easy to see whether you agreed with mostly right-brain or left-brain statements. But if your answers seem to conflict, then you're in the enviable position of being pretty balanced.

Knowing these answers will help you to improve your written work. In Chapter 2 you'll set goals based on these answers. So, make sure you feel you've evaluated yourself in the most accurate way. Right-brain people tend to know what they mean but can't get it onto paper. Left-brain students can write in a logical way but sometimes lack inspiration and stick to facts or rote learning.

So, how exactly do we get to whole-brain writing?

The best writing uses an integrated approach. In writing it is the left brain that pays attention to mechanics such as spelling, agreement and punctuation. But the right side pays attention to coherence and meaning; that is, your right brain tells you it 'feels' right.

According to some experts, the trick is not to try and get out of your left brain and into your right but instead to increase activity in the right hemisphere (or reduce activity in the left) so it matches the activity on the other side. To be truly creative, you need to be balanced.

This book covers both left-brain and right-brain activities. With this knowledge, you'll be better equipped to figure out how best to improve your writing. You don't need to worry about this too much as the exercises in the book create a balanced programme. However, here are some simple tips to start thinking about straight away:

- To get the right brain working, try and create images in your head while you're working and actively increase your use of metaphors, analogies and visuals.
- To activate the left brain, you need to plan and structure your work, actively think about what techniques you're using and edit as you go along.

Your writing MOT

By now, you should have learnt a lot about yourself as a writer. Here's the chance to summarize it, in handy format. In the UK, cars older than three years have to go through a yearly MOT (a Ministry of Transport test) where a trained mechanic goes through a list of checks to see whether it is road worthy. This is very similar to what we've just done. So, here's your MOT summary sheet. Think of this as a checklist that will help to keep your writing machine in good working order.

Constructive thinking (write out the thoughts and beliefs you have about writing that are helpful)

____

____

Destructive thinking (write out the thoughts and beliefs you have about writing that are unhelpful and that you want to change)

Right brain versus left brain (summarize your results from the quiz: write out any statements that really rang true for you)

- Do you prefer facts or ideas?

- Are you a thinker or a feeler?

- Are you more structured or flexible?

Your writing types (state the writing types – such as Perfectionist Petra and Fun-seeking Fehmina – that you identified with)

Areas for improvement (summarize the areas of writing you want to improve)

What next? (list the actions you're going to take over the next 30 days)

____

____

____

____

____

____

This information is invaluable as we progress to the later stages of the book. For instance, if you're a thinking type and you're writing a very emotional, tragic case study, you may want to include some feeling-type language to make it more effective.

Using a variety of techniques, tools and quizzes, this chapter has found out what kind of writer you are, and your likes and dislikes, so that you can best tailor the rest of the programme to you.

We all have preferences. Some of us like chocolate ice cream, others butterscotch mixed in with strawberry, while some can't stand all that gooey stuff and would much rather have a pastry. When it comes to writing, it really is no different. Except that if you don't know your preferences and don't understand what type of writer you are, writing can be really hard, like climbing up a steep mountain incline barefoot without a harness.

You now have real tools to start to think yourself into the fantastic writer you really are. You can also periodically revisit this chapter and amend your MOT and the answers to the other questions as you progress and develop as a writer. This section can grow with you and provide you with a strong foundation from which to write.

Further reading

You can find out more about your personality type by using the Myers-Briggs Type Indicator. Visit www.myersbriggs.org.

Student Comment

Paulina, French and Philosophy undergraduate
Writing types: Perfectionist Petra and One-Trick Oliver

'I loved the fact that the first chapter was very engaging and really made you think about your attitude to writing. Many writing books just give you exercises and tell you what to write, which can make you wonder whether it is at all helpful or suitable to you. It was great to really feel like I would be working for my own needs, rather than following general instructions. It was fun and exciting to get involved straight away!'

What do you hate most about writing and why?
I hate not being able to find the right words or expressions (or metaphors and similes) to express what I want to say. I hate not knowing my own style and being scared of experimenting because of feeling like 'I'm not good enough'. It takes a lot of time to get to something that I really like or am proud of, but because of my initial fear, I am unwilling to put the time in for fear of just wasting my time!

Paulina's affirmations to help combat these writing dislikes:

1 I can write quickly and effortlessly
2 I can express myself well in writing
3 I have a fantastic style of writing
4 My writing is creative and interesting
5 I can begin an assignment without delay

Greta says:

'In Chapter 4 we'll learn the technique of object writing, which will help your metaphors and similes to flow more easily and help you to write in the moment and use your first instinct, rather than trying to second guess yourself, or be critical. This will also help you overcome your perfectionist tendencies and try out new ways of writing. You'll also learn a really easy technique for choosing the exact metaphor or simile that fits what you want to say. This will help your essays to run more smoothly.'

Chapter 2

Aim for victory with goal setting

Having completed Chapter 1, you now know exactly where you are as a writer. Your Global Positioning System (GPS) is flashing. Now you need to input it, not only with an end destination but some signposts along the way.

So in this chapter, you'll work out where you want to go and why. I'll also map out the key behavioural signposts along the way that will tell you you're on the right track. If you're getting itchy feet because we haven't done any writing composition yet, it's still worth resisting the temptation to skip ahead. This is because setting goals sets you up for success. You won't achieve every single goal you set yourself, but you give yourself a fighting chance by doing so.

A recent study at Dominican University found that 43 per cent of people who wrote down their goals achieved them (Dominican University 2008). The act of writing stimulates the reticular activating system (RAS) in the brain. The RAS is like a filter and it sorts the things that are written down as being important. Of course, it's likely that you also write down things such as 'buy baked beans and butter' when compiling a shopping list, but writing down goals helps you to focus on them, and get grounded and realistic about them.

But that's not all. People who went one step further and shared their goals with a friend and sent them weekly updates were 33 per cent more successful in accomplishing their goals. So make sure you find a tutor, study partner or roommate to share your goals with.

Quiz: What type of goal setter are you?

The first step is to analyse your attitudes to goals, success and failure. Fill in the quiz below. There are no right or wrong answers; the aim is to get to the bottom of your current goal-setting behaviour.

When did you last set a study goal?

____

____

____

What motivated you to do so?

____

____

____

Did you achieve it? If yes, give reasons why. If no, explain why you failed.

____

____

____

What do goals mean to you?

____

____

____

How does your writing type (for example, Fun-seeking Fehmina) affect the way you set and achieve goals?

____

____

____

The 'F' word

Whether you feel that goal setting is a chore, a nice-to-have or an integral part of your life and studies, the chances are good that your goal-setting attitude has a lot to do with your relationship with the 'F' word. Failure is an emotionally charged word. Instead of striving for success, many students do all they can to avoid failure – two very different sets of actions and states of mind. At university, failure is usually equated with a poor grade. But it's important to look at the actions behind the supposed 'failure' and then change course to avoid them in future.

In fact, it's often necessary to fail forward. This is failure, or bad grades, that teaches you something vitally important that ensures that in the future you achieve success. In order to escape mediocrity it's necessary to fail, because if you're not failing then you're not trying new things.

The paradox is that if you fail forward in this book, you have a greater chance of developing the writing skills that will improve your grades overall. In every student I have worked with, improving writing skills automatically improved their grades, irrespective of their knowledge or understanding of the subject.

It's true that setting goals can be stressful as it puts pressure on you to succeed. But goals can also help you to feel more positive about your skills and abilities and achieve more satisfaction in your university work.

Some study questions

Before you set your goals, let's take a further look at where you are now. These questions are very open-ended, and there are no right or wrong answers.

What are three writing-related challenges you are facing right now?

____

____

____

____

____

What's the one major thing that holds you back from being an excellent writer?

____

____

What one skill would have the greatest impact on your writing?

What additional people, groups, resources and organizations do you need to help you improve?

Take further stock of where you are by gathering together all the practical things you need to enable you to summarize where you are with your writing. These can be past essays, reports, notes, feedback sheets and research. Look at the comments and suggestions and try and pick holes in your own work. Where did you go wrong with your writing and why? What would you do differently in the future?

The exercise that you've just completed contains the kinds of questions that your university tutors will ask you to fill in as part of a Personal Development Plan (PDP) for your degree. These plans ask you to state:

- your personal learning objectives for a set period;
- the departmental objectives that your personal objectives feed into;
- what you will do to meet the objectives;
- when you have to achieve them;
- whose support you'll need;
- how you'll recognize success.

What motivates you?

Now you need to create a vision of how you see yourself, your writing and your future. Ask yourself the following questions:

What is my purpose for following this book?

____

____

____

How will my life be different at the end of it?

____

____

____

My main reason for improving my writing is:

____

____

____

____

____

The SMART way to set goals

Now we'll get down to the nitty-gritty – actually setting your goals. Use the SMART acronym which has been shown to be the smart way to set goals. Your goals ought to be:

S Specific

M Measurable

A Achievable

R Realistic

T Timed

Specific

Don't say that you want to do well in your exams; say that you want to achieve an 85 per cent average.

Measurable

Make sure that you can tell when you've reached your goal. For instance, if you want to be more confident in writing, you could measure this by the time taken to complete an essay or the fact that you produce a draft of an essay without constantly crossing things out. Write your goals in terms of these measurable actions.

Achievable

You must believe that you have a shot at achieving the goals you set yourself. However, this doesn't mean that you should lower the bar and not aim high. On the contrary, you should aim as high as possible, but you should also know that – with a stretch – you can achieve the goal. If the goal seems far too big or too much of a stretch, you're likely to become disillusioned and fail to reach it.

Realistic

Being realistic means making sure that you're aware of your highest potential. For example, if you are dyslexic or have a learning difficulty then achieving second-class marks may be your highest potential if your course is heavily essay-based.

Timed

Finally, if your goal doesn't have a time limit then it's simply a wish or a dream rather than a goal. Make sure you set a date by which you will achieve it. Setting a date also helps you to focus as it gives you something to work towards.

Goal sheet

Now it's over to you. Write down three goals you want to achieve in the next month, and at least one goal you want to achieve in the next three months, six months, 12 months, three years and five years. This enables you to see how your short-term goals link into your long-term goals. Use this goal sheet to create your writing goals and remember to use the SMART format. If you're having trouble thinking of goals, look back to your answers to the writing MOT in Chapter 1 for inspiration.

Here are some examples of SMART goals:

- It is May 2012 and I am completing my end of term essay with ease. I am writing freely with very few crossings out and even smiling while doing so.
- It is March 2013 and I have published an article in my university newspaper.
- It is September 2013 and my innovative dissertation idea has been approved by my tutor.

One month

____

____

____

Three months

____

____

____

Six months

____

____

____

One year

____

____

____

Three years

____

____

____

Five years

____

____

____

Remember, the process of goal setting should be an ongoing one. Your goals ought to shift and change over time – and as you work through this book. Once you have achieved your goals, think about where you want to go to next, and write out new goals. Keep setting small goals and achieving them. Then you can work towards bigger and bigger success.

You can also go one step further and model your PDP by creating a formal plan for your writing skills progression. See the end of the chapter for a further resource on this. But in any case, make sure you use a calendar or diary to write in specific actions you will take on a daily, weekly or monthly basis that will enable you to reach your goals.

Student Comment

Margaret, Economics undergraduate
Writing types: Perfectionist Petra and Last-minute Lorraine
A sample of Margaret's goals:
Six months: It is December 2012 and I am writing a cover letter for a position I wish to apply for with little effort and within three hours.
Three years: It is July 2015 and I am a confident writer who has completed half of my dissertation.

'Perfectionist Petra affects my goals by causing me to be far too ambitious. I am then faced with having to work towards goals which are far beyond my writing capabilities. When I don't achieve the goals I set myself I'm always so disappointed. I know this is all so unnecessary but I find it hard to stop myself doing it. I am now trying to set realistic goals I feel comfortable with.'

Developing emotional intelligence

As you set, plan and work towards your goals you'll need to develop or enhance your emotional intelligence. When you think of intelligence, it's likely that you'll think of prowess in maths or science. Emotional intelligence (EQ), though, is something that everyone can develop. Put simply, it's being able to manage the emotions of yourself and others. According to Daniel Goleman (1995), it's made up of four elements: self-awareness, self-management, social awareness and relationship management. The part we need to focus on is self-management – controlling your emotions and impulses and being able to adapt to changing circumstances.

In fact, reading a degree can be seen as one long emotion-management programme. You've got to develop the self-discipline necessary to keep going, the tenacity to try a little harder when things seem hopeless, the ability to take criticism and the dynamism to change the way you approach work with the aim of getting better results.

Seven steps to a higher EQ

1 Use positive self-talk

This means speaking to yourself in a kind, caring way. Many of us are not aware of our own inner dialogues. Think about the last time you failed at something, or didn't do your best. Did you say something like, 'I always mess up!' or, 'Why am I so stupid?'

This kind of talk just makes you feel bad about yourself. Take inspiration from the affirmations you created in Chapter 1 and think about positive self-statements instead. So when things go wrong or you find something difficult, say, 'That was hard; I did really well for tackling it and not giving up.'

2 **Create positive pictures**

Create positive pictures in your mind of yourself passing exams, writing winning essays or achieving first-class marks. Dwelling on future success rather than future failure (even if you fail) will help you feel positive about yourself and your work. It will also help you to create a more positive study environment.

3 **Develop persistence**

Persistence means putting aside frustration when something goes wrong. If you mess up, keep trying. Lots of small improvements over the course of the year can dramatically improve your work.

4 **Be determined**

You need both determination and persistence to succeed. You can persist at something in a very half-hearted way, but if you add determination you will be unstoppable. Determination is having such a strong desire to do something that you will not let anyone stop you – even when it becomes difficult.

5 **Hone your self-belief**

It doesn't matter what grade or results you're currently getting, make sure you believe that you are capable of achieving greater success.

6 **Take responsibility**

Never put the power of your achievements in other people's hands. So even if you think a lecturer, study partner or librarian didn't pull their weight in helping you, always remember that *you* alone are ultimately responsible for your success.

7 **Make a habit of asking questions**

If you don't know something – ask. It's the best way to learn. And it's a habit that will make you bright and successful. Asking good questions means you get good answers and it will stop you from going through university with gaps in your knowledge.

Dealing with obstacles

So you've figured out your motivation for improving your writing, set your goals and strived for the best personality traits. The final thing to remember here is that there will be obstacles along the road to success. For example, if you fail a paper or misunderstand a research project, you're not going to do yourself justice. But if you plan for blips in the road then you won't be completely floored by them.

It can also help to write about the obstacles that you're facing. A recent study found that writing about emotional topics not only helped people to feel better but also helped them to improve their grades and even secure new jobs (Pennebaker and Chueng 2007). So, think about writing as being far more than a means to an end – it can help you achieve more than the degree of your choice.

Further reading

Cottrell, S. ([2003] 2010) *Skills for Success: The Personal Development Planning Handbook*. Palgrave Study Skills, Palgrave.

Student Comment

Sara, English Literature undergraduate

'It is difficult to make long-term goals because I don't know how things will turn out. I'm short of money at the moment and don't know if I will be able to continue my studies.'

Greta says:

'It can be difficult to set realistic goals and stick to them, especially when you don't know what steps to take to achieve your one-, three- and five-year goals. One way to combat this is to assume that everything will take twice as long as you originally think it will. This can help you be more realistic. And if you don't know what steps it will take to reach a goal, just invent some. For example, if you want a job at a publishing house, you may want to start with a search of all the publishing houses in your area. You may also want to read stories of famous publishers for inspiration. Take whatever steps you like, as taking action encourages you to take more action, which will eventually produce results.

But if you're finding it impossible because you don't know what the future holds, then set two sets of long-term goals, one for if the future turns out one way, and one if it turns out another. Imagine different possibilities for yourself and set goals based on those. Alternatively, set more general goals that you are certain you can achieve, irrespective of what the future holds.'

Chapter 3

Read your way to writing

Unless you've been blessed with a photographic memory, it's unlikely that you remember the mechanics of learning to read. But around the age of 5, you began using picture cues and repeating stories you'd heard. Next, you learned to read in phrases instead of word by word, and connected your own experiences to reading. And so it went on, until you one day found yourself in the university library with a reading list so long that you felt like the protagonist in Munch's seminal painting *The Scream*!

At university, you're expected to read widely and independently. But instead of outlining research tips, the crux of this chapter is getting to grips with the way you read – with a view to learning writing skills. That starts by putting aside your required reading list. Your prime motivation for reading set material is to extract knowledge that can be used in essays and exams. However, this pragmatic approach doesn't help you to understand how texts are structured, or learn about style and technique. But if you actively read well-written texts, you can start to emulate authors and transform the way *you* write.

Exercise: Be a voracious reader

The first step is to get in the habit of reading whatever words come your way, no matter where you are or what you're doing. This way, you build your reading muscles day by day.

Let's begin with a simple (but not always easy) exercise. For the next week, keep a notepad and pen with you and note down every time you read a fun, snappy phrase. It doesn't matter what it is or where you read it. It could be a leaflet in the student union, a billboard advert in town or your cereal packet. It could be in a magazine, newspaper or even a text book. As long as you think it's fun and fresh – write it down. Aim to find 10 favourite phrases from different sources.

To get you inspired, below is an example from my student Paulina. Use the same headings when you complete the exercise.

Type of reading material: Milk carton

Title: Oat milk

Where I was when I read it: In the kitchen

Favourite words and phrases: Ode to oats

The aim of the exercise is to show that there is excellent writing all around you, and the more you read it, the better chance you have of learning the skills behind it. What's more, it took Paulina just a few seconds to read the milk carton – so you too can devour words wherever you go. Don't worry if at first you find it hard to find any favourite words or phrases in anything you read, or if everything seems uninspiring. Just keep your eyes open and you will start to look at language in a different way. By the end of the week, you will start to see simple words in new ways.

Master pencil power

Next we're going to explore active reading, using magazine articles which are (in most cases) easier to digest than books and essays. The easiest way to begin reading actively is to use pencil strokes on the text as you read. This may seem simplistic but making concrete marks out of abstract, unarticulated thoughts while reading helps to engage and focus your brain.

Exercise: Active reading

Choose a magazine or journal that is related to the degree you're studying. For instance, if you're studying economics, you could opt for *The Economist* or if you're studying nursing, you could choose *Nursing Standard*. Pick your favourite article and make a photocopy of it. Read through it once to get a sense of what it's about. Then grab a pencil and annotate the text using the active reading and literary techniques checklists below. The idea is to train yourself that all reading goes hand in hand with deep questioning and thinking. So, when following the checklists, make sure you:

- underline key points, phrases and words;
- write down your thoughts, comments and questions;
- record every reaction you have.

Active reading checklist

The title

What is significant about the title? Why has the writer chosen it?

Purpose and theme

What is the purpose of the article? What messages is the writer trying to convey?

Structure and facts

Why have the facts been pieced together in the way they have? Is there anything unusual about the structure of the article?

Surprises

Are there any surprises in the data, arguments, issues or story? What significance do these have for the topics being discussed?

Unusual words

What unusual words are there? Why has the writer deliberately chosen these over simpler or more obvious words? What effect do these words have? If you come across any words you don't understand, look them up in a dictionary and write out their meanings.

Your reaction

What is your opinion on the topics discussed? Do you agree or disagree with the writer? How would you approach the issues differently?

Tone and mood

What thoughts and feelings does the article create in you? Is the article cynical, hopeful, cruel, happy or sad, for instance? Why has the writer chosen to adopt a particular tone?

Literary techniques checklist

In order to create imagery, writers use literary techniques. When using the checklist below, identify why the writer has chosen a particular technique or used a particular image.

Metaphors and similes

Has the writer described one thing as being another? For instance, 'Science is the gateway to understanding' or, 'London is like a melting pot.' Notice that the first example is a metaphor and the second is a simile.

Alliteration

Has the writer used two or more words in a sentence that begin with the same consonant? For instance, 'Brazil is a riotous clash of cultures.' What effect does this have? How does it make the words and ideas come alive?

Personification

Have any objects been described using human qualities? For instance, 'The river argues and bellows its way downstream.'

Symbolism

Has a person, place or thing been used to represent something else? For instance, a canary in a cage can represent entrapment or a person refusing to reveal his or her true self.

Irony

Has a situation been described where the opposite of what is expected to happen, happens? For instance, it's ironic that valuable, rare, raw materials can be extracted from industrial waste.

Sibilance

Has the writer used two or more words in a sentence that begin or end with the letter 'S'? For instance, 'senseless snobbery' or, 'The waves were bliss.' What effect does this have? How does it make the words and ideas come alive?

Onomatopoeia

Has the writer used any words that sound the same as the real sound, such as 'bang', 'crash' or 'wallop'? For instance, 'The test for hydrogen is the squeaky pop test.'

Repetition

Has the writer repeated ideas, sentences or phrases deliberately for effect? For instance, 'Churchill was a man of great character, a man of wisdom and a man of authority.' What effect does this have?

The overall purpose of using literary techniques is to draw attention to words, phrases and sentences in a creative way. They make writing more exciting and interesting so that the events jump off the page. They also help to create pictures in your mind that make you want to read more. Pay particular attention to how these literary techniques have been used, as the aim is to emulate these in your own writing – with the help of this book, of course. You'll begin this process in the next chapter.

Don't worry if you find some of the things in the checklists hard. Sometimes you won't know what the theme is, or you'll find hardly anything to tick off. This is fine. The goal is for you to read actively in a whole-brained way and simply using the checklists will help. Eventually, this type of reading may become second nature. But for now, and as you follow this book, grab that pencil and keep annotating.

Openings and endings

Newspaper and magazine articles are very cleverly structured. They hook you with the opening statement or paragraph, take you on a journey throughout and then end in a provocative or interesting way. The end of the article often makes reference in some way, shape or form to the beginning but it shows how the writer, character or issue has moved on. There always has to be progression. And there's usually something witty, or something to make the reader think. The best essays also use these same techniques.

Here's a rundown of the most common introductions and conclusions used in articles and essays.

Article and essay introductions

Story in a snapshot

This is literally a whole story in no more than a few sentences. The story usually involves something highly interesting and unusual.

The element of surprise

This can be a surprising statement, question, fact, statistic or opinion. The crucial component is that it catches the reader off-guard.

A blast from the past

This technique looks to history – whether distant or recent – and describes or sums up something interesting that has happened.

The way it is

This technique simply describes a person, place or thing – it presents it like it is. In essays, this technique works well when the writer defines a term or concept.

From the horse's mouth

This opening is the use of a quote, which can be someone telling a 'story in a snapshot', using 'the element of surprise', giving 'a blast from the past' or sharing 'the way it is'. This technique is especially effective when the person being quoted has great authority or influence.

Reporting the news

In this technique, the introduction begins by reporting something newsworthy, that is, something that has recently happened and is of great interest. This technique only works with articles, not essays.

Article and essay conclusions

Round-up, round-up

This is simply a summary of the issues and ideas already discussed in the article, presented in a new and fresh way.

Crystal ball gazing

In this technique, the article ends with a prediction about the future. This could be a warning or a positive picture of how things will turn out. In an essay, this could outline avenues for future research.

From the horse's mouth (in summary)

This is the same technique as 'from the horse's mouth' above. The only difference is that its purpose is to use the quote as a summary or prediction, or to shed new light on the issues discussed in some way, shape or form – perhaps also using 'the element of surprise'. The 'element of surprise' can also be used on its own as a conclusion.

Of course, when you're reading you may not find the introductions and conclusions laid out exactly as I have presented them here. In introductions, for instance, writers sometimes combine various techniques to create a 'puzzle' that the readers have to solve, more fully present a problem or achieve a greater sense of closure. Make sure you pay attention to all the introductions and conclusions you come across as the best way to learn how to write your own is to copy these techniques from other writers.

Exercise: Media montage

Choose five magazine articles and see if you can spot the introductions and conclusions that the author has used and why. Try and choose articles from a variety of sources such as trade magazines, newspaper supplements, consumer magazines and supermarket magazines. These magazines don't have to be related to your degree as the idea is to explore a range of different writing styles and topics. If you're short on options, you could ask your friends or roommates if they have any magazines you can borrow. Alternatively, visit your university library and have a good rummage.

Below is an example from my student Emily, who analysed an article called 'We need to reduce our noise footprint', from the *Guardian* newspaper. Use the same headings as she has when analysing the articles.

This exercise will greatly help you when you come to write your own articles and essays. And every time you pick up an article from now on, start to think about how the writer has constructed it and why.

Table 3.1 Emily's article analysis

	Text	*Techniques used*	*Why?*
Introduction	'My dad was such a noisy riser that, a few years ago, I wrote a song about it because it was a ritual that was stamped on to my soul [. . .] his slippers made more noise than tap shoes across the landing'	Story in a snapshot	Opening the article with a funny, personal story effectively draws the reader into a more serious issue
Conclusion	'So let's make today the day we reduce our noise footprint, even slightly. A great journey begins with a single step. In slippers of course'	Crystal ball gazing and the element of surprise	The writer hopes to inspire us to take action but he includes the surprising element of the slippers, which wittily links back to the opening story about his dad. Again, this lightens the mood of a serious topic

Source: McMillan 2010

Exercise: Expanding into essays

Essays are written in a more formal style than articles and so, on the whole, a good essay writer will use the introduction and conclusion techniques in a less creative way – unless writing an argumentative or explorative essay. Your task is to see if you can spot the use of the techniques in essays. This will make it easier for you to try out these techniques yourself later in the book, when writing your own essays. So, which techniques have been used in the following five introductions and two conclusions? The excerpts may use more than one technique and the answers are at the end of the chapter.

To remind you, the techniques are:

- Story in a snapshot
- The element of surprise
- A blast from the past
- The way it is
- From the horse's mouth
- Reporting the news
- Round-up, round-up
- Crystal ball gazing

Introductions

1 The Health and Safety at Work Act (1974) stipulates the rules and regulations for ensuring a safe workplace. However, the number of occupational diseases is increasing. In 2007, there were 8.6 confirmed cases of occupational disease for every 100,000 people employed. In 2008, this rose to 13.3 (WSH Council 2008).

2 Genre is 'a complex pattern of repeated social activity and rhetorical performance arising in response to a recurrent situation' (Paré and Smart 1994). In this view, genre goes far beyond a written discourse.

3 For Type 2 diabetes, a dietician may recommend patients consume probiotic foods such as live yoghurt, or fermented foods such as sauerkraut and kefir. They may also recommend a probiotic supplement in addition to the standard advice of lowering calories and fat.

4 During my school placement observation, I came across a Year 10 student with a misconception. When the student was asked what an electron is, his response was, 'It is energy.' When he was asked what energy is, he responded by saying, 'It is electrons.' He had no correct definition of either an electron or energy.

5 Celie was vulnerable when she married as a child. However, she grew up to be a strong woman, able to follow her own path and escape from a violent marriage.

Conclusions

1 The costly nature of conducting nutrigenomic testing means the NHS would be unlikely to offer it (Human Genetics Commission 2009). There

is also the dilemma of which groups to target for routine screening should it be introduced. Furthermore, there may simply not be enough resources to meet the needs of patients with increased risk.

2 It seems that the innovative efforts of companies to improve their financial performance and the environment simultaneously will create a 'win–win' situation.

A new way to read essays

By now you may be thinking, 'Wow – I *almost* like essays now, but I couldn't possibly swallow a whole one!' But that is exactly what you're going to do in the rest of this chapter! One of the best ways to do this is to read books of essays. In your library, there will be books of essays on every subject from physics to post-war feminism. These books will be housed under the banner of literary non-fiction. Put simply, literary non-fiction is fact-based writing that uses elements of fiction, poetry, memoir and essay. It tells stories, puts data into context and gives insight into facts.

The types of essays you will write throughout university are unlikely to be those of the literary non-fiction kind. But reading them is an accessible way to explore essay writing techniques. What's more, these types of essays are entertaining and lighter than a straight thesis on postmodernist discourse, for instance. They allow you to read complex arguments and see how rich information can be conveyed in compelling, persuasive ways.

Exercise: Bursts of active reading

Your task is to find two books of essays that are directly related to the degree subject you're reading. Make sure you choose books that are interesting and capture your imagination. So, do some detective work, both in the library and on the internet. One word of warning though: don't be tempted to read text books. These are instruction-focused pieces of writing aimed to impart knowledge, not demonstrate a point of view, persuade or provoke within a set format. Each day for two weeks, set aside 10 minutes for active reading. Choose an extract from your book and use the checklists (on pp. 38–40) to actively read the text.

Exercise: Plotting the arguments or narrative

Now, take one of your favourite chapters from your book and look at how the writer has laid out the arguments, or structured the story, if the text is more literary. Answer the following questions:

What is the 'story' of the chapter?

What arguments or issues does the author present? How? And in what order?

What are the author's main viewpoints? Do these change? If so, why?

Is the author balanced or biased towards a particular viewpoint?

What type of introduction and conclusion has the author used and why?

____

____

____

What techniques has the author used that you might want to copy in your own work?

____

____

____

Active reading leads to vibrant writing

By forcing yourself to slow down long enough to read actively you can learn a great deal about how to write. So, don't put aside your books, magazines and journals just because this chapter is over. Continue to be a voracious and, above all, active reader.

Answers: Expanding into essays

Introductions

1 The element of surprise, the way it is and blast from the past

2 From the horse's mouth

3 The way it is

4 Story in a snapshot

5 The way it is

Conclusions

1 Round-up, round-up

2 Crystal ball gazing

Further reading

There are no firm prescriptions here on what books to read for the exercises, but remember if you're choosing fiction you'll learn more by going for books written by 'literary greats'. However, if you simply want something to help you extract information for essays and other documents, the following book will help.

Fairbairn, G. and Fairbairn, S. (2001) *Reading at University: A Guide for Students*. Open University Press.

Student Comment

Zenna, Psychology undergraduate

'I really enjoyed the media montage exercise. It was a lot of fun reading through different types of magazines and actively engaging with the texts. By the fifth article I was starting to spot good and bad writing techniques, and even evaluating why they are so. This will be invaluable for my own writing.'

Greta says:

'The important thing to remember in this chapter is not to be afraid to "steal" techniques that you read in other writers' work. This is completely different from plagiarizing, which is stealing content and passing it off as your own. Keep learning how other writers structure their work and make good use of the techniques in the active reading and literary techniques checklists and emulate them.'

Part II

Creative tools and writing techniques

Chapter 4

Write with objects

So, you've devoured the work of others (while working through the previous chapter) and learnt how to spot the use of particular writing skills techniques. But you may still find it a struggle to get your *own* thoughts down on paper. So if you've ever felt blocked or stifled when writing, the exercises in this chapter will help. You'll also learn how to use literary techniques in your own work. This chapter is a complete right-brain workout that will loosen you up and get your words flowing on the page. If you're already very right-brained – and find that your writing already flows – these exercises will still help, and will enable you to focus your creative energies. They also pave the way for the more analytical, structured techniques that are to follow in this book.

The main technique we're going to use is called object writing. It was originally invented by Pat Pattison (a Professor at Berklee College of Music) in order to help songwriters write better lyrics (Pattison 1995). But it's not just songwriters who can benefit from using this technique – it has helped all my students in their academic writing and can completely transform *your* writing skills. It increases your powers of description, which is useful when writing essays and articles. And it also increases your ability to give quick examples, stories and analogies that will bring your writing to life. What's more, if you're having difficulty getting started, it can kick your writing muscles into fifth gear. It's easy to master, fun, and gives fast results. This can help you build the confidence you need to tackle more difficult pieces of writing. And it doesn't matter which objects you write about, the power is in the process of using the technique.

What is object writing?

Put simply, it involves taking an object and writing about it using *only* your seven senses. So, you look at – or imagine – the object and focus on what you can see, hear, touch, taste and smell, the movement of the object and how you feel about it. You then do this in short bursts of 90 seconds, five minutes or 10 minutes.

Most of you are familiar with the first five senses but it takes a little extra practice to describe objects in terms of feeling and movement. Think about feeling as being more than just your emotions. For instance, does an object (and your associations with it) make your heart beat faster, or your muscles tense up? When it comes to movement, don't just think of the obvious movement an object makes. Instead, think about your internal movement, when interacting with the object, such as the strange sensation you get when back on solid land after being on a theme park ride.

Sample object writing

Here is an example of object writing. Notice that not all of the sensory descriptions are written in full sentences. That is, there is not a verb in every sentence. In object writing (and object writing alone), this is fine as the aim is to work your creative muscles, not to produce grammatically perfect prose.

Peach – 10 minutes

The plump juicy globes are ripening in the summer sun. Swirls of orange, like countries of the world, are blended with coral and yellow on an artist's palette. Blended so effortlessly that no one knows where they begin or end, merging seamlessly, proficient and masterful. None of that painting by numbers, this is the real deal.

And just taking a bite, as tart, tangy juice runs down my chin caught opportunistically by my tongue savouring the fresh, just picked taste. Forgetting my peach's journey across country, across state and finally across the bustling market, wheel barrowed to my favourite stall and handed to me like an offering at church. My hands touch the grainy flesh smoothed as though it were touched by sandpaper, until just a hint of roughness remains indelible. Yet the roughness there leaves an imprint, like Bach flower remedies diluted and diluted until almost nothing is there but a whisper in a deadened ear.

Teeth marks surround the bitten flesh as though they mark a territory for no one else to touch. No sharing, no passing around – this is a treat for one. I want to devour it all in one go, but politeness seeks a napkin, folded delicately, separating the peach from my hand, as though it were sacrilege to touch the now adulterated flesh. As the napkin mops the juice from my chin, the peach inside is fresh and inviting. Scores of yellow-orange flesh pieces nestle together in strands, like millions of yellow men with their hands held high.

I pause and then bite and bite and chew and chew, swallowing concoctions of fruit glory – a symphony of passion and purpose. Inhaling aromas of velvet vanilla, tinged with bergamot as though tasting fine wine, or working as a nose. Deep in my laboratory testing smells for their potency and allure. And I wonder how to crush the peach into a bottle, as I've just crushed it in my mouth. Then sell it for £5 and bring smiles to the faces of the world. That would be just peachy. Just peachy and everything would be alright.

Six steps to great object writing

1 Write, or type, the following headings at the top of the page to remind you of the senses you need to focus on:

   See *Hear* *Touch* *Taste* *Smell* *Move* *Feel*

2 Grab a stop watch and set it for 90 seconds, five minutes or 10 minutes.

3 Begin spontaneously writing down whatever comes to mind about the object. Aim to write from a place of excitement and interest and be as specific as possible with your descriptions and images.

4 You don't need to stay completely focused on the object, so don't worry if random words and sentences tumble out. Just go wherever your seven senses lead you.

5 Write in full sentences if you can but don't worry if you're writing in phrases, where you use adjectives instead of verbs.

6 Above all, keep your hand moving across the page and don't stop to cross out words or correct spelling mistakes. Only amend spellings, grammar errors or any other mistakes when you're finished. And don't worry if your writing appears clunky and disorganized. You'll work on refining your writing later on in the book.

Exercise: Your first piece of object writing

For this exercise you'll need a piece of fruit of your choice. Examine the fruit carefully – smell it, taste it and touch it. Listen to the sound it makes when you take a bite; the movement when you chew and chomp and any feelings that arise. Then do a 10-minute object writing session about it.

Focus, focus, focus

If you found the object writing exercise hard and had trouble getting down on the page what you really wanted to say, then go back to Chapter 1 and see which writing types you identified with. For example, if you were a Fun-seeking Fehmina, then perhaps you approached the exercise half-heartedly. Next time, deliberately concentrate as though your life depended on it.

If you identified with Perfectionist Petra, then you might have been afraid to write messily and quickly. You may have written far less than you could have and used 'safe' words and images. If this is you, then remember that you're not ever going to be graded on this work. It's a fun exercise and you'll get the most benefit from being as messy and free-thinking as possible. In contrast, if you identified with Slapdash Simon, you might want to slow down a little and take more care.

Answer the following questions:

What were your writing types, as identified in Chapter 1?

____

____

____

____

What strategies can you create to make your writing types work for you?

____

____

____

How to hit a home run

While you're consulting Chapter 1, look at your answers to the questions about whether you preferred the following left-brain or right-brain traits:

Left-brain traits	*Right-brain traits*
Facts	Ideas
Thoughts	Feelings
Scheduled	Flexible

If you prefer facts over ideas, then deliberately avoid using facts in your object writing and stick to ideas. For example, instead of saying, 'The peach is pink inside', write 'The peach is the colour of ballet slippers.' The first example is a fact because it can be verified, the second is an idea; no jury can categorically say whether the inside of a peach is in fact the colour of ballet slippers.

Similarly, if you prefer feelings, try to include more thoughts. So instead of writing, 'The peach makes me feel happy and giddy', write 'It was picked in Paris from a large orchard.' And if you know that you're a planned, organized person, try to make your writing spontaneous – and vice versa. Do your best to try out new ways of writing.

Remember, object writing is an exercise you want to play with and have fun with. Writing needs both left-brain and right-brain skills so ensure you learn how to manipulate yours. But whatever you do, never forget that object writing is about expansion – you want to amass as many words as possible. Think of it like rolling a large ball of clay. The more clay you have the more you'll be able to chip away later to create a beautiful piece of prose. And the great thing about object writing is that it's really enjoyable and you'll get a huge feeling of achievement from regularly accessing your senses and producing interesting and exciting descriptions.

Your daily object writing workout

Spend the next 90 days doing daily object writing. It's up to you whether you choose to work every day or just five days a week, but for your first 30 days, choose a different object each work day and write for 10 minutes per day. Don't try to edit or correct anything, just enjoy the work you produce.

For the following 30 days, choose a different object each day and write for five minutes per day. Finally, for the last 30 days do 90-second bursts of writing using a different object each day. Aim to really focus in the 90-second bursts so that you can get the maximum amount on the page in the shortest time possible.

After each session, go over your work and underline your favourite images. Here are some examples of images from my students' object writing:

- The river bellows
- We pull tissues from boxes like magicians doing tricks

- The colour of blushing cheeks
- Two intertwined C's glaring at me with expectation

Throughout your 90 days of object writing, make sure you continue to work through the rest of this chapter, and the rest of this book. Each day's object will help you with all the exercises that follow. Try not to write when you're in a rush or in a noisy, hectic place. Instead, set aside a time and place where you can work best. This exercise will show you that you can write interesting, lively pieces in a very short period of time. Try your best to use the objects as laid out here, but if the odd one or two don't resonate or make sense for you, use an object of your choice.

These are such quick bursts of writing that there's no way you can argue that you don't have time to do them. Better still, do them with a friend. There's nothing like setting a stop watch together to get you focused. By reading your work aloud to each other, you get a different perspective on the object. This can help you to be even more creative and confident, especially if your friend tells you how much they love your images.

90 objects, 90 days

You can do these objects in any order – just tick each one when it's finished.

10 minutes		
Balloon	Fountain pen	River
Beach	Briefcase	Restaurant
Wedding dress	Picture frame	Sunglasses
Diary	Speedboat	Iron
Banana	Atlas	Hospital
Park	Baby	Car
Lipstick	Theatre	Flowers
Disco	Television	Computer
Celebrity	Train	Horse
Funfair	Swimming pool	Letter
Five minutes		
Jet ski	Hair	Packed lunch
Knife and fork	Taxi	Mobile phone
Hat	Scarf	Box of tissues
Office	Wallet	Umbrella

Tea bag	Painting	Bicycle
Shopping centre	Running shoe	Football
Shark	Wig	Poster
Tattoo	Motorbike	Raincoat
Piano	Teapot	Rice
Rocking chair	Box	Moustache
90 seconds		
Fizzy drink can	Xylophone	Watch
Test tube	Envelope	Piggy bank
Dining table	Sun lounger	Magazine
Tennis racket	Spice rack	Video game
Bottle	Fly	Vase
Brick	Light bulb	Broom
Dustbin	Soap	Perfume
Cellar	Rat	Handshake
Aeroplane	Pebble	Stuffed toy
Candle	Songbook	Water

Do a debrief

After each 30-day period, look at how your writing behaviour has changed and ask yourself the following questions:

How has my writing improved?

___

___

___

What can I do better?

___

___

___

How can I make my writing more whole-brained?

____

____

____

Am I writing freely and easily? If not, why not?

____

____

____

How can I make this process even more enjoyable?

____

____

____

Exercise: Practising literary techniques

In Chapter 3, you practised spotting literary techniques. Now, by doing your object writing it's likely that you have spontaneously used them yourself. This is because focusing on your senses helps you to create the kind of word pictures that are used in the literary techniques.

Go through your favourite words and phrases that you underlined after doing each piece of object writing. Try and find an example of each of the following literary techniques:

- Metaphors and similes
- Alliteration
- Personification
- Symbolism
- Irony
- Sibilance
- Onomatopoeia
- Repetition

If you can't find an example of each of these, take a phrase which is almost there and deliberately craft it so that it uses the technique.

Here are some examples from my student Paulina:

Table 4.1 Paulina's list of literary techniques

Object	*Literary technique*
Pine tree	Personification: The pine tree stands tall and proud
Bookshop	Simile: It is like stepping into a cave which transports you back in time
Letter	Alliteration: Messy masses of paper
Apple	Onomatopoeia: Thud! The large green apple falls from the tree

The no-frills guide to metaphors

So you've got your senses flowing, honed your powers of description and explored literary techniques in greater detail. Now, it's time to go one step further and focus on metaphors. When you were reading essays in Chapter 3, you may have noticed that many of the writers used metaphors. This is because metaphors make it easier to describe complex things. When you talk about abstract things in the language of things you're comfortable with, they are easier to communicate and understand.

What's your MQ?

Metaphor quotient (MQ) is a term that was first coined by American dancer and creativity coach, Twyla Tharp (2007). But to explain what it is, it helps to compare it with intelligence quotient (IQ).

Most of you will be familiar with the term IQ – when someone is really smart, we tend to say they have a high IQ. There are lots of intelligence tests that measure IQ. These usually involve solving word or mathematical problems. They're designed to test how well you can think in a logical, rational fashion. And afterwards you're given a score to determine whether you're average, gifted, genius, or, in fact, the next Einstein.

However, instead of measuring your reasoning skills, MQ measures your creativity skills. It's about how skilled and gifted you are in creating metaphors. By improving your MQ, you'll find that demanding tasks such as writing essays will be much easier. You should find it much simpler to explain your points and be analytical. This is because you'll be fully practised in comparing things and finding interesting ways to express your ideas. When you have a high MQ, the detail in your writing becomes fresh and vibrant – but most of all original.

Exercise: Creating a metaphor table

This method is also inspired by songwriting Professor Pat Pattison and is a simple way to create metaphors. First, take an object. You can use one of the ones listed earlier in this chapter, or pick your own. Keep your object in mind and ask yourself two questions:

1 What qualities does my object have?
2 What else has those qualities? This can be an object, concept or person.

Then describe the word as if it were actually that object, concept or person. The easiest way to do this is to create a table. See Tables 4.2 and 4.3 for examples.

Table 4.2 Paulina's first metaphor table

Object	*Qualities*	*What else?*
Sunrise	Bright, slow, soft, orange, glowing, yellow, energizing, early	Pastels, light bulb, snail, jewels, an orange, birds

Chosen metaphor: The **sunrise** was a **snail** gliding upwards into the sky

Table 4.3 Paulina's second metaphor table

Object	*Qualities*	*What else?*
Computer	Grey, black, plastic, metal, square, technological, artificial, intelligent, complicated, useful, necessary, tiring	Box, scientist, genius, women, child, robot

Chosen metaphor: The **computer** was a cunning **child** demanding constant attention

Finally, choose three objects of your own and repeat the whole process by creating tables of your own and using them to create metaphors. Write your chosen metaphors below:

1 ____________________

2 ____________________

3 ____________________

Playing with your metaphors

Once you have some metaphors, see if you can express them in different ways. This works best if both your object and the thing you are comparing it to are nouns. For example: using the nouns 'mind' and 'blank slate', you can express the metaphors in three different ways.

1 The mind is a blank slate
2 The blank slate of the mind
3 The mind's blank slate

See how many ways you can express your current metaphors and then choose three nouns of your own and express them in the three ways above.

____

____

____

____

After a while this process will become second nature and you won't need to draw tables or actively think of lists of verbs and nouns.

Beyond objects to academic voice

Each person is unique and we all use our senses in slightly different ways. This is great news for our writing. It means that we all approach words in slightly different ways. When you use your senses, you tap into your unique powers of writing. Your work can become boldly different from everyone else and you develop what experts call a 'writer's voice'. This is when people can recognize that you're the author of a piece of work without your name being on it. You can apply object writing to any document you need to write. Apply the principles to academic concepts and ideas to free up your writing and enable you to be bold in the way you express your ideas.

Further reading

Pattison, P. (1995) *Writing Better Lyrics: The Essential Guide to Powerful Songwriting – From Ideas to Developing Verse and Beyond.* Writer's Digest Books.

Goldberg, N. (2005) *Writing Down the Bones: Freeing the Writer Within.* Shambhala Publications Inc.

Student Comment

Emily, Pharmacy undergraduate
90-second object writing on a fizzy drink can

Shake it if you dare. Put it in the freezer for hours if you dare. Flick it open and . . . a spray of foam shoots high up like a volcano exploding. Erupting into the sky and falling into my hair. The sweet, sticky liquid runs down my cheek and I take a little lick.

'In object writing you are continuously writing, so whatever image or idea comes to mind, you write it down. Once completed, you can pick out the phrases and sentences that you feel sound the best. Overall, this has helped me discover ways of writing that I didn't know I was capable of.'

Ginny, Management Studies graduate

'It's great that you refer back to the writing types that we identified with in the first chapter. It's helpful to be able to understand why an exercise was hard or easy and how to improve on this. I found all of the exercises on metaphors absolutely brilliant and extremely useful. I have a hard time coming up with metaphors so this chapter really helped. Until now, I didn't know that there were practical techniques I could use to improve my writing. I used to think good writing skills were something you were born with.'

Greta says:

'Each time I work with students on object writing, literary techniques and creating metaphors, they are amazed at how freely they are able to write. They are also surprised by releasing latent abilities they didn't know they had. Each student finds that they can be creative and write interesting pieces that are uniquely different from anyone else's. This is essential in laying the foundations for expanding on your thinking and turning this into effective essays and other documents.'

Chapter 5

Your toolkit of techniques

Law undergraduate Amir was looking for a quick essay-writing fix, so I gave him one tip: make effective use of linking words. He duly followed my advice and saw his usual grade of a lower second jump to an upper second. Can it really be that simple? The answer is yes *and* no. Of course, you'll need a base of skills on which to add specific techniques. But you should have already developed that in Parts I and II of this book. So, now you need to bridge the gap between the creative writing you did in the last chapter and the focused, academic work that your lecturers demand from you. To do this, you need to learn a series of writing skills techniques.

The techniques you'll learn in this chapter are extremely powerful. Learn and master them, and you will see results. So, here's a rundown of both formal and informal techniques, including when and where you should use them. If you're ever unsure about a particular document, and are unable to ask your lecturer (or another expert), it's best to use a more formal technique.

ALL-PURPOSE TOOLKIT

These tools are universal – so use them in every document you write.

Audience tracker

The first thing to do before writing any document is to think about who will read it. There should never be a 'one size fits all' policy. Your writing and the style and structure of your document need to change depending on who will read it.

Asking yourself the following questions will help you to focus on your readers and prioritize the information you want to include:

- Who are my readers?
- How much do they know about the subject/issues I am writing about?
- How important is my document to the readers?
- What will my readers look for in my document?
- What is the most important thing to include?
- What type of data or supporting evidence do my readers value?
- What do I want the readers to do, say, feel and think after they've read my document?

If your document is not important to your readers and they know little about the issues discussed in it, you'll have to work harder to gain their attention. On the flip side, if they're extremely knowledgeable about what you're writing, it helps if you can shed new light on the topic or present it in an interesting way.

Just one sentence

Being able to sum up the purpose of your document or its main message in one sentence is very powerful. This is because it enables you to have a crystal clear focus before you begin the planning and writing process. This technique will be invaluable if you use it before you write *anything*. When you know your main message, it's easy for even the longest document to have laser sharp focus. Use it in conjunction with the audience tracker technique.

Exercise: Short and sweet

Here are some exercises to help you to practise distilling your thoughts into just one sentence. The first is borrowed from a writing competition run by American magazine, *SMITH* (SMITH 2012). The magazine asked readers to write their life story in just *six* words. When doing this exercise, my student Emily wrote, 'Still waiting to get a pet', while Margaret wrote, 'Found once-in-a-lifetime love.'

Write your life story in six words

____

____

Choose your favourite book and think about the plot. Now describe it using just one sentence.

____

____

Describe a complex concept, idea or study from your university course in just one sentence.

____

____

The exercises above take a lot of hard thinking and require you to write down lots of information before editing it down to either six words or just one sentence. To do this successfully, you have to take a stance. Choose an angle you want to take and focus on that.

Active voice (with occasional use of the passive voice)

All writing has a voice, which is either active or passive. This book is largely written in the active voice but many of the essays and journals you'll read for your degree will be written in the passive voice. 'Voice' simply refers to the grammatical structure of each individual sentence. The passive voice focuses on the action (or thing) and not the person doing it. It can be difficult to read as the crux of the sentence is always at the end. Your reader almost has to process everything twice and so passive sentences can seem jarred and stilted. They can also make your writing very vague.

In contrast, the active voice focuses on the person (or thing) and not the action they are doing. It helps keep the text lively, which engages the reader. Here is an example of each:

Passive	*Active*
Fifty health posts were established in rural Ethiopian villages in 2011.	**Help Children International established fifty health posts in rural Ethiopian villages in 2011.**

When to be passive

The passive voice is useful if you don't know (or don't want the readers to know) who's doing the action. It's also useful if the people or things are too numerous to list, for example, 'Over 14 additives were used in the apple pie.' Also use it when you want to emphasize the object in the sentence, for example, 'An estimated 33 trains are boarded in London each minute.'

It's also customary to write some scientific documents, such as psychology reports, in the passive voice. So, you should double check with your lecturer before making all documents active. But where the two voices are interchangeable, it's always better to use the active voice.

Exercise: From passive to active

Rewrite these sentences using the active voice

The elections were supported by a government-funded programme.

____

____

Each year, an estimated 17 million deaths worldwide are caused by coronary heart disease.

____

____

Verbs instead of nouns

In the passive voice, sentences are often constructed around a noun instead of a verb. This means that the sentence focuses on the name of the action, instead of the action itself. For example, 'The creation of a new health post was undertaken by the government' uses the noun 'creation' when it could use the verb 'create'. In this case it would read, 'The government created a new health post.' Verbs give sentences movement and life, so where possible aim to construct yours around them.

Exercise: From nouns to verbs

Rewrite each sentence in Table 5.1 so that it's constructed around the verb (using either the past or present tense). The table shows the corresponding verb for each noun, and includes a sentence constructed around the noun.

Table 5.1 From nouns to verbs

Noun	*Verb*	*Sentence*
Consideration	Consider	The consideration of GDP is essential when determining a country's prosperity.
Election	Elect	The election of child parliamentarians by Maputo City took place in 54 schools.
Recommendation	Recommend	Smith gave the recommendation that the National Theatre expand its programme.
Provision	Provide	The provision of facilities management services is undertaken by an external agency.
Decision	Decide	The General Medical Council took the decision to strike off the doctor.

Keep it simple

Try not to use words just to look smart or prove that you have a large vocabulary. If you do this, then it's difficult to truly express what you want to say and your writing will lack depth. Instead, choose the word that best expresses exactly what you want to say. And unless academic jargon is essential, don't be afraid to use simple words.

An excellent way to write in a simple, clear, concise and spontaneous way is to write as though you were talking to your best friend. By doing this, you bypass the urge to try to be clever, write like a professor or sound as though you've swallowed the entire works of Shakespeare. You will also be able to bypass the voice in your head that tells you your writing is no good. This works so well, that for some of my students it's been the technique that has transformed their writing the most. Try it for yourself in the next document you write – it works.

Being specific

Don't use general statements in your writing if you can be specific. For example, don't write that there are many rivers in Egypt, but state how many there are. Here is a simple way of getting your work to be as specific as possible.

When you have finished a document, read through it carefully and ask yourself if any of the information is incomplete. Do this by writing one or more of the questions 'who?', 'what?', 'where?', 'when?', 'why?' or 'how?' next to the incomplete information. For example: 'China may not be the communist country it once was; however, the theatre is still restricted by the government.' Why? How? If you apply this technique thoroughly, you should be left with questions all over your document, which should prompt you to find more evidence, information or examples to make your work more specific.

Exercise: Specifying your object writing

The aim of this exercise is to practise making phrases more and more specific by combining creative techniques with extra research. At university you'll have to find specific evidence to back up anything you write, so this exercise is one step towards doing that. The aim is to ensure that what you have written is both narrow and expressive, in that it combines the full facts with sensory/creative expression.

So, go back to your object writing from Chapter 4 and pick three or four of your favourite phrases or sentences. Now research some specific, factual information that you can use in conjunction with them. For example, if your phrase was, 'The children, mouths sore from hunger, swallow the swollen rice' you could find specific statistics or studies about the number of starving children in the world, or the science behind what happens when a person's mouth literally swells from hunger.

Below is an example from psychology undergraduate Irina. Structure your answers in the same way.

Object: Tea pot

Phrase: With engravings and drawings along its fat belly, the samovar is more like an art piece, or an antique belonging to another era, rather than a pot for making a hot drink.

Research: Samovars are functional devices made of iron, tin, copper or other types of metal. Some are plain but others have painted folk motifs. If you visit Russia, it's likely you'll see Samovars on trains, in traditional restaurants or at parties.

New phrase: With folk motif engravings along its fat copper belly, this samovar is like an antique belonging to an ancient Russian era.

Short sentences and phrases

Long, rambling sentences are difficult to read and understand, so avoid using them wherever possible. Aim for around 25 words per sentence. If you're struggling to keep your sentences short, it could be that your thinking is fuzzy. Alternatively, you may simply need to use more full stops.

Exercise: From long to short

Rewrite this into three shorter sentences of around 20 words each. Use the active voice and substitute nouns for verbs.

The achievement of carbon savings of up to 30 per cent is possible if drivers simply adopt a more relaxed driving attitude in terms of planning their braking and accelerating to be as smooth as possible and adequately maintaining their vehicles by ensuring that ignition and fuel flow systems are efficient and tyre pressures are optimal.

____

____

____

The use of especially short sentences is also a technique in itself. Short sentences are great for highlighting ideas. For instance, in a philosophy essay, Paulina began with, 'An old proverb states that there is no disputing over taste. This means that each person has his preferences and arguments over taste often lead nowhere, because no individual can be persuaded to like something they detest. Or so it seems.' By placing a longer sentence next to a highly short one, the information in the short sentence is spotlighted. The focus remains on 'or so it seems'.

Exercise: In the spotlight

Choose a concept, idea or theory related to your degree. Deliberately write sentences of around 25 words followed by a short one for effect. Ask yourself why the information in the short sentence should be put in spotlights. If you're not sure why then rewrite your sentences until your strongest message is contained in the short sentence. The short sentence should be up to 10 words. This technique is also useful when writing personal statements and compiling CVs, cover letters and other 'selling' material. In this instance, you could write down your best qualities and spotlight the ones you think are most important to land you the job.

Pick 'n' mix linking words

Linking words are joining words and phrases that connect ideas together. They can make a dramatic difference to your writing, not least because they help your reader to believe that you have a coherent argument. Here is a list below:

- However
- On the other hand
- It seems that
- It is possible
- It may be that
- Perhaps
- At least
- Although
- Once again
- Finally
- Then
- In contrast

- If
- Most importantly
- So long as
- Similarly
- Even though
- This suggests that
- The analogy of
- From one point of view
- It can be argued that

You can begin paragraphs with linking words and use them when you're evaluating points and presenting different points of view. Practise using them when writing so that you create a style that you're comfortable with.

Rewriting, editing and proofreading

Great writing is not written, but rewritten. And if you compared the first and last drafts of your favourite books you'd find that they were very different. If you're doing a creative piece of writing, the main thing to remember is that you should only rewrite, edit and proofread once you've completely finished the brainstorming and 'creative' part of your writing. Just as in your object writing, aim to write continuously without too many crossings-out, and then go back later to refine your document.

However, if you've been assigned an essay or another highly academic piece, it's better to approach the writing process in a cyclical way where your writing is interspersed with periods of research, thinking, editing and rewriting. It'll be virtually impossible to creatively channel a whole piece of writing as you can with personal documents and even articles.

Rewriting

Rewriting is about looking at each sentence and deciding whether you've written it in the most effective way possible. This could involve changing the theme or deleting whole paragraphs and writing them again.

Editing

Editing is about shifting around the structure of the work. You could change the order of sentences, paragraphs and arguments to make the document as snappy and interesting as possible. When editing, ask yourself the question, 'So what?' If you can't answer this, then the message of your document isn't compelling enough. When editing, make sure every word counts by crossing out unnecessary words.

For most university documents, it's not appropriate to get someone else to edit your work after you. But for any other documents that are going 'public' like CVs, cover letters and personal statements, make sure that you're not the last person to see them. Getting a second pair of eyes can give you a completely fresh perspective.

Proofreading

Proofreading involves checking that you haven't made any spelling, grammar or punctuation errors. So this is the very last step in the writing process. Use your spell checker but don't be a slave to it. Your Microsoft spell checker doesn't have all the answers, so Bill Gates cannot be held responsible for any slip-ups! This is because spell checkers read for accuracy, not context, and so they don't know the difference between angle and angel, for example. What's more, they can't always fix clunky phrases, typos and grammar mistakes.

It's more difficult to read words on a screen, so print out a hard copy too. Then use a pencil and stop it at every word to slow your brain down. This is because our eyes often see what they want to see instead of the words on the page. It also helps to put your work to one side for at least a day. Then when you come to it again, it will be fresh and you should be able to spot the mistakes immediately, especially if you read it aloud.

Checking strategy

After rewriting, editing and proofreading, check your work for accuracy. Spend time checking all the details, including facts, figures, names, dates and references. If you need help with referencing, see the further reading section for an excellent resource on writing with sources. Finally, check your work for sense. Does it make sense? If you don't understand things, you can be sure your reader won't either.

TOOLS FOR FORMAL DOCUMENTS

Use these tools for essays, dissertations and reports.

Formal words and phrases

There are undoubtedly specific words and phrases that relate to your degree, so make sure you know these and are comfortable using them. For example,

Business and Finance uses terms such as 'smoothing', 'arbitration' and 'cap and collar rate'. Law uses Latin phrases such as 'locus in quo' and 'nota bene' and International Development Studies speaks in terms of 'advocacy', 'social mobilization' and 'community participation'.

Exercise: Keep your own dictionary

Every time you see a new word or phrase, write it down along with its plain English equivalent. Instead of being daunted by new terms, begin to develop a curiosity for them. This exercise can be ongoing, so buy a special notebook and keep it handy whenever you're reading or attending lectures or seminars.

Create a table, following the same format as Table 5.2. In the plain English column you should put the clear, straightforward English equivalent (not slang or street talk!). This exercise will help you to develop a formal vocabulary, but it will also help you when you need to write informally, as you'll have also identified the informal alternatives to formal words.

Table 5.2 Example of dictionary: formal words and phrases with their plain English equivalents

Plain English	*Formal, academic equivalent*
Emotion	Affect
Discussion	Discourse
Heart attack	Myocardial infarction

Formal linking words

We've already looked at general linking words that you can pick 'n' mix for use in any document. But here's a list of the main formal linking words that can be used in essays, dissertations and reports:

- Therefore
- Thus
- Furthermore
- Moreover

- Indeed
- Nevertheless

Third person viewpoint

Sentences typically use one of three viewpoints: first, second or third. The third person uses the words 'he', 'she', 'it' and 'one'. For example, 'It can be seen that there is a clear progression in status between 2009 and 2010.' This viewpoint gives a formal tone, so always use it in essays, dissertations and reports. But as with any rules, there are certain times when you'll need to break it:

- Avoid the third person in personal essays and informal reports.
- If you're studying science, ask your lecturers if they want you to write your lab report in the first person or third person.
- Avoid using 'one' where possible as it can sound a little too much like Her Royal Highness Queen Elizabeth II. And I imagine that this is not the tone of voice you're trying to convey in your written work! If you're struggling to be opinionated while still writing in the third person, avoid writing 'In one's opinion . . .'. Instead, simply state the opinion or write 'It can be argued that', or 'The author argues'.

Effective use of evidence

For your arguments to be taken seriously, you need proof. So don't be tempted to make assertions if you don't have the evidence to back them up. Evidence can be quotations, facts, figures, statistics and studies. But they must come from a credible source. And for every piece of evidence you find, you have to tell the reader where it came from.

At the bottom of the credibility pile is Wikipedia and at the top are peer-reviewed journals. But depending on your degree, you might use quotes from *The New York Times*, a country's census or even online film and TV reviews. Be aware that adverts and company-sponsored research are biased sources of evidence as they have been commissioned to support a point of view or sell a particular product. So make sure you choose evidence where you know the writer or researcher has no hidden (or unhidden) agenda. If in doubt, ask your lecturer where you should go in search of evidence.

Evidence is not like salt and pepper – so don't just sprinkle it around liberally. You have to carefully put it in places where it helps the reader to understand the argument or issue. The rule is to make a statement, give evidence and then explain it. The aim is to slowly pile each piece of evidence on top of the last until you have a watertight argument, or, in the case of an essay, you have effectively answered the question.

Exercise: Choose your evidential angle

Below are three pieces of evidence. Write an introductory statement for each, insert the piece of evidence and then make up an explanation for it.

- Geda found that in 70- to 89-year-olds, the higher the number of calories consumed, the higher the likelihood of developing mild cognitive impairment (MCI) (Geda *et al.* 2012).
- Describing Christianity, Hume states: 'Our most holy religion is founded on faith, not reason' (Hume [1758] 2012).
- According to Westwood *et al.*, there are 3.5 million women in managerial and professional positions in the UK (Westwood *et al.* 2000).

The aim of the exercise is to show you that it's not the evidence that gives weight in a piece of writing; it's what you use it to show or suggest. Different people will put these pieces of evidence in different contexts depending on what they interpret.

Here is an example from Pharmacy undergraduate Emily, using the second piece of evidence:

> It can be argued that all religions are based solely on beliefs, and therefore do not need to be underpinned by evidence. Describing Christianity, Hume states, 'Our most holy religion is founded on faith, not reason' (Hume [1758] 2012). However, if religions cannot be explained logically, there must be additional forces at work which account for why individuals convert from one faith to another.

And remember that although this is listed as a formal tool, you can – of course – use evidence in informal documents. However, it doesn't have to be referenced, and it can consist of your own thoughts, senses and observations rather than the objective facts.

TOOLS FOR INFORMAL DOCUMENTS

Use these tools for articles, speeches, PowerPoint presentations, action plans, portfolios and other more informal documents.

Informal words and phrases

Informal words and phrases are everyday words (also called colloquialisms) that are used in unrestrained speech. In contrast to the serious tone of formal words and phrases, their main purpose is to create a light, fun, fresh, friendly, chatty or witty tone. And they certainly spice up writing. Contractions (such as 'mustn't', 'didn't' and 'haven't') are informal and can be used alongside this technique. Their formal counterparts (such as 'must not', 'did not' and 'have not') should always be used in formal documents.

Table 5.3 Some formal phrases and their corresponding colloquialisms

Formal phrase	*Colloquialism*
Give me a call	Give me a bell
It is an excellent movie	It's an ace movie
It was a big lie	It was a huge fib
Visit the surgery	Pop into the surgery
Luxurious new restaurant	Swanky new restaurant
Very different from her sister	A far cry from her sister
Jamie tried a new concept with his new recipe book	Jamie broke the mould with his new recipe book
It is not important	It's not a big deal

Exercise: From formal to free speech

Your task is to see what colloquialisms of your own you can come up with (see Table 5.3 for some examples). The aim of this exercise is to prevent your writing from being on a default setting that you have no control of. Don't worry if you can't think of any off the top of your head though. Look through whatever reading material you have to hand, whether it's a novel, a text book or a gossip magazine. All these types of documents use different types of words and phrases, and you may spot some colloquialisms you want to use, or use the material as the starting point for developing informal alternatives to formal words. To inspire you, here are some colloquialisms from my student Margaret:

- Din-dins
- Bog standard

- You have made a pig's ear of that
- Bucketing down

Write 10 of your own below:

1 ______________________

2 ______________________

3 ______________________

4 ______________________

5 ______________________

6 ______________________

7 ______________________

8 ______________________

9 ______________________

10 ______________________

Plays on words

Words can sound similar but actually have two meanings and deliberately mixing these up can create humour. The official term for this play-on-words technique is 'pun'. And puns are often used for dramatic effect in newspaper headlines. You'll find them useful when you come to write your own articles – in particular headlines and subheads.

Here are two examples of puns and their context.

Pun:	*Context:*
From Russia with gloves (Bloomberg Businessweek 2010)	This is a play on words taken from the title of the James Bond film, *From Russia with Love*. It was used in a business article about white-collar boxing.

Much ado about muffin at BA (Wheeler 2007)	This is a play on words taken from the title of the Shakespeare play, *Much Ado about Nothing*. It was used in a tabloid article that described how a British Airways steward was suspended for theft after he took a muffin left by a passenger.

Exercise: Now pun it!

Look online at newspaper and magazine headlines and aim to find five plays on words. Explain the context in which each has been used.

First-person, second-person and imperative viewpoint

The first person uses the words 'I', 'we', 'us' and 'our'. For example, 'We can see that there has been a clear progression in status between 2009 and 2010.' The second person uses the words 'you' and 'your'. For example, 'When you read a novel, it can help to expand your awareness of people with different lives to your own.' There's also the imperative which uses none of these and simply gives instructions, such as, 'Mix 8oz of flour with three eggs.'

Use the first person when writing Personal Development Plans, articles, speeches and portfolios. Use the second person (as well as the first person) when you want to talk directly to your reader, in job applications, personal statements and informal magazine articles. You can also use the second person in informal reports and both the second person and imperative when giving instructions.

Exercise: Object perspective

Again, revisit your object writing and choose two of your favourite sentences. Rewrite them using the first-, second- and third-person viewpoints.

Informal linking words

Here's a list of the main linking words that can be used in informal documents:

- So
- Also
- What's more
- In addition to
- But
- In fact
- In any case
- Anyway

The power of three

On 20 January 1981, when US President Ronald Reagan gave his First Inaugural Address, he said, 'This administration's objective will be a *healthy, vigorous, growing* economy.' (Bartleby.com 1989). The three words in italics used in short succession use a technique called the power of three. This is where you use three adjectives or phrases to get your point across. This technique is very effective when used in speeches. You can also use it in cover letters and personal statements. It creates balance, which helps to drive a message home. But use it sparingly. Don't litter the power of three all over your work; instead, carefully place it for effect.

Exercise: Speech-finding

Go on the internet and find some speeches. Speeches by politicians are good as these will have been written by professional speechwriters. Find six examples of the power of three and write them below. Next to each example, use that particular power of three in a sentence of your own. You can find a wealth of speeches at www.ted.com.

1 ____

____

____

2 ____

____

3 __________

4 __________

5 __________

6 __________

Mixing formal and informal tools

There are times when you'll need to combine the formal and informal tools. For example, use formal techniques for documents such as personal statements, CVs and cover letters, but write your personal statement and cover letter in the first person and include the second person in your cover letter. Again, if you're ever unsure, ask your lecturer for advice.

Putting it all together

Take heart, as you may find it difficult and even downright shaky at first as you try to implement new ways of writing. But if you keep practising you'll see noticeable results very quickly. Keep practising these techniques before moving onto Part III of this book. Once you've mastered the lessons in this chapter, you'll find it easier to express the ideas you'll brainstorm in the following thinking exercises.

Think of this chapter as being a reference guide of writing techniques that you revisit again and again. And when you come to Part IV of this book, where you apply your knowledge to different documents, you should actively incorporate everything you've learnt in this chapter and the previous ones.

Further reading

These books go one step further in outlining the technical aspects of writing. The third book is a punctuation and grammar workout.

Peck, J. and Coyle, M. ([2005] 2012) *The Student's Guide to Writing*. Palgrave.
Harvey, G. (2008) *Writing with Sources: A Guide for Students*. Hackett.
Dignall, C. (2011) *Can You Eat, Shoot and Leave?* Collins.

Suggested answers to selected exercises

From passive to active

- A government-funded programme supported the elections.
- Each year, coronary heart disease causes an estimated 17 million deaths worldwide.

From nouns to verbs

- It is essential to consider GDP when determining a country's prosperity.
- Maputo City elected child parliamentarians in 54 schools.
- Smith recommended that the National Theatre expand its programme.
- An external agency provides the facilities management services.
- The General Medical Council decided to strike off the doctor.

From long to short

It is possible for drivers to achieve carbon savings of up to 30 per cent if they simply adopt a more relaxed driving attitude. This includes planning their braking and accelerating to be as smooth as possible and adequately maintaining their vehicles. Drivers need to ensure their vehicles have efficient ignition and fuel flow systems and that tyres are at the optimal pressure.

Greta says:

'The answers above are for the exercises that can be marked "right" or "wrong". But many of the other techniques are more subjective and so you just need to practise implementing them using the guidelines in this chapter.'

Part III

Thinking like a genius

Chapter 6

How to think up grand ideas

How good are you at thinking things through? Have you ever been taught how to do this? And if you have, by whom? The thinking skills movement can be traced back more than a century and there has been much academic research on thinking. But it's unlikely that you've been actively taught it – and almost certainly not in relation to writing skills.

In fact, with almost every student, out of the hundreds I've worked with, when I ask the question, 'What do *you* think?' the default answer is usually 'I don't know.' But it's not that they don't know, it's just that they've never really thought about their opinions before. When I work one-to-one with students on their writing, a lot of the sessions involve thinking and talking. I have found that when students become confident in their thinking abilities, the content of their writing dramatically improves and so do their grades.

Researchers have also found that mastering thinking skills improves academic performance. But it's not just your ability to think about a particular topic that causes the improvement. For example, Adey and Shayer (1993) researched high school students who received thinking skills teaching, as part of their science lessons. These students not only scored on average a grade higher in their science exams than a control group, but they did significantly better in all their other exams too.

Many of you will have found that education up until now has placed more importance on memorizing facts than maintaining curiosity, as means of ensuring you achieve good exam grades. Yet, you're expected to arrive at university with your high-level thinking processes intact. And these are then expected to flourish independently due to wider reading, seminars and lively discussions among your fellow students in the Student Union bar.

It's rarely that simple. We're socialized to believe that knowledge and intelligence is about memorizing and old habits can die hard. It's only with gentle coaxing and teaching of specific thinking techniques that you can really open up your imagination and your capacity for abstract thoughts and reasoning.

Active thinking is not easy. We all have default ways of thinking that become routine so that they are no longer active. Thinking in particular ways strengthens the neural pathways in the brain making a type of thinking *even* more likely. Previously learned ways of thinking (and behaving) become automatic, such as driving a car, walking to work, writing an essay and taking an exam. The challenge lies in waking and shaking up your thought processes.

The good news is that, whatever your natural thinking preference, you can work towards whole-brain (or genius) thinking. When you think of the word genius, it's likely that someone such as Einstein comes to mind, as for many people he's the text book example of a genius. But in fact, a genius is someone who effortlessly integrates left- and right-brain thinking. In the language of the previous chapters, this is someone with both a high metaphor quotient (MQ) and a high intelligence quotient (IQ).

This chapter will show you how you can work towards attaining genius status! It's a great workout for your thinking muscles. The aim is to prepare your thought processes for the more intense writing tasks that you'll tackle later in this book, and at university and beyond.

Left versus right

Left-brain thinking is about putting thoughts and ideas into separate categories. This type of thinking involves recognizing a pre-defined system or pattern, or trying to predict a system or pattern. It's about breaking problems down into their constituent parts, weighing up opinions and arguments, being critical and looking beyond the surface to what's really going on. In contrast, right-brain thinking is about finding connections and similarities between ideas and using metaphors and symbols to help do this.

Thinking about 1+1

Table 6.1 is a summary table (with examples) of some different types of left- and right-brain thinking in response to the question 'What is the significance of 1+1?'

Exercise: Practising thinking types

Using the different types of thinking in Table 6.1, create your own table based on the question, 'What is the "good" life, for individuals?'

Which types of thinking did you most resonate with? If you're more of a left-brain thinker, your challenge is to make way for intuitions or hunches to come along (I'll describe how later in the chapter). If you're more right-brained, you need to make logical and analytical sense of your diverse ideas and impulses.

Table 6.1 The different types of left- and right-brain thinking

Left-brain thinking	*Right-brain thinking*
Logical	**Metaphorical**
1+1 = 2	1 + 1 creates two united warriors in the world.
Rule-based	**Free from rules**
To get the number 2, you have to use addition, subtraction, multiplication or division.	You can arrive at the number 2 by a variety of creative means.
Exact	**Ambiguous**
The properties of the number 2 are precise and finite.	The number 2 is greater than the sum of its parts.
Based in reality	**Based on intuition**
This sum has been presented by experts as the best one to suit our needs.	This is not the right sum to ask in this instance.
Practical	**Symbolic**
The sum 1+1 is an effective means of teaching people the rudiments of arithmetic.	The sum 1 + 1 symbolizes a balanced, harmonious marriage.
Analytical/Critical	**Explorative**
In presenting this sum, the writer has not explained what the numbers represent. The numbers take on a new significance depending on whether they are objects, people or concepts.	The concept of one person must be loosely defined. Some people have large families and communities supporting them. Others are literally alone in the world. So, how can 1+1 always equal 2?

Towards whole-brain thinking

Mind maps are a great tool for promoting integrated left- and right-brained thinking. This is because they stimulate both sides of the brain. These maps are simple to draw and are useful for everything from planning essays, to finding original ideas or revising for exams.

How to draw a mind map

1 Take a large sheet of paper and draw a circle in the middle. Inside write the topic that you want to explore further.

2 Next draw a line from the circle and write the first thing that comes to mind. This can be a keyword, phrase or sentence.

3 Keep drawing legs from the circle that correspond with what you brainstorm, and draw additional legs at the end of legs to show ideas that relate to one another.

4 Repeat steps two and three until you have exhausted all possibilities.

5 If you find yourself getting stuck in the thinking process, think about the question and then ask yourself, 'who?', 'what?', 'where?', 'when?', 'why?' and 'how?'

6 You can also put yourself in another's shoes. Ask yourself, 'What would an artist say?' or, 'What would an inventor say?'

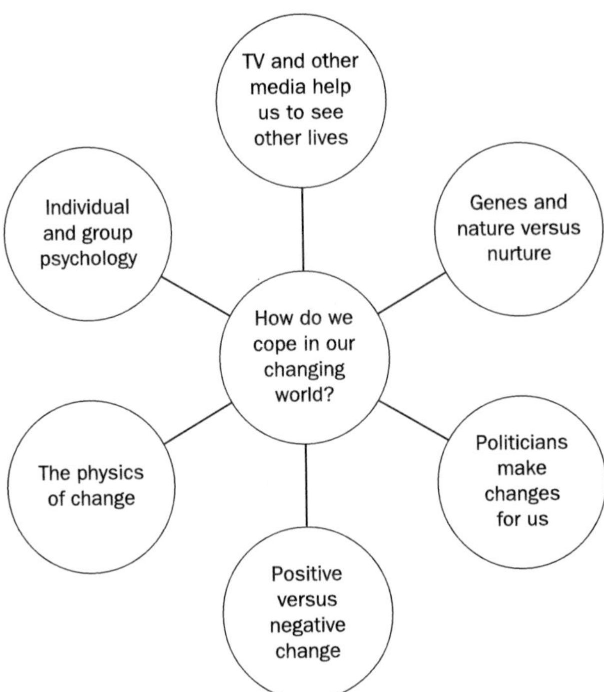

Figure 6.1 Example of a mind map

7 To further expand your thinking, keep asking yourself, 'What else?' But don't be satisfied with the first, second or even third 'what else' answers you come up with. Keep pushing yourself.

Notice in Figure 6.1 that the six outer circles represent only the first layer of thinking. In your mind maps you need to expand on each circle several times. Think of it as being like a giant family tree with branches and sub-branches that go back centuries. When you're drawing mind maps, don't be afraid to come up with lots of wild or wacky ideas. The best way to get good ideas is to get lots of ideas, and then throw the bad ones away. So don't judge anything you write during the brainstorming process.

Exercise: Applying a mind map

Below are some general philosophical dilemmas that the world's leading thinkers have been pondering for decades. Choose a question and draw a mind map based on your thoughts about the question. Next, write a role play between right-brained thinker Tom, who is a visual artist, and left-brained thinker Bryony, who is an IT consultant. Use as many of the thinking types in Table 6.1 as possible.

Here are the questions:

- Is there a universal truth that applies to everyone, or is truth relative?
- Is life governed by fate or free will?
- Who decides good or bad, right and wrong, and by what standards?
- What place do people have in the universe?

These questions may not seem especially creative but your task is to make them so. I have chosen these questions as they are broad enough for students of any discipline to answer.

Exercise: Integrating MQ and IQ

Go back to the questions in the 'Applying a mind map' exercise. Pick another question and draw a mind map aiming to use as many of the different

thinking types as possible. After you've completed this, choose the question that you feel has generated the most interesting mind map and write a short 500 word mini-essay that answers it.

To get the full benefit of this exercise, aim to combine everything you've learnt so far in this book. Here are some further guidelines to help you do this:

- Go back to Chapter 3 and look at the article and essay openings you identified. Choose two or three of them and practise crafting short introductions using the techniques. For example, English undergraduate Anna looked at the issue of fate versus free will. She began her mini-essay with a quote from author C.S. Lewis and then used a metaphor, describing fate as being God's puppet strings. She described the world as containing 'seven billion puppets all smacking their wooden palms together'.
- Remember to combine the lessons from Chapter 4 here. So, choose a key word from the question and do a 10-minute object writing session on it.
- Make full use of metaphors. Pick a word or phrase from your mind map and draw a metaphor table based on it. Then include a sentence (or paragraph) based on this metaphor.
- Avoid beginning with a definition – you can define the terms after you've begun the mini-essay. But it can help to look up all the key words in the question in the dictionary, as this can spark some creative ideas.
- Try to question assumptions. So imagine that your answers are like an onion where each layer gets to the heart of the issue and ask, 'What's beneath this?' and 'What's at the heart of this issue?'
- Ask yourself the question, 'What if?' Then brainstorm six playful and explorative 'What if?' questions that get you thinking further about the issues. For example, 'What if we had a telepathic pen that wrote down our thoughts?' The best ideas are generated by being willing to embrace ambiguity, paradox and uncertainty. So don't worry if your questions seem silly – just practise being creative.
- You can find an example from your own life that relates to the question and start writing from there in the first person. Describe this and then relate it back to the question. You can always change this to the third person, if you like, later.
- There are no right or wrong answers to these questions. Simply argue for and against, giving examples and reasons why.

- Finally, as this is a thinking exercise, you don't need to do further reading, find references or quote other academics. The aim is to unleash the creative and logical thinking already lying dormant within you.

Breaking through dead-ends

All the thinking you've been doing in this chapter has been pretty intense. So don't worry if it feels like your brain is seizing up or going on strike. It's not pleasant if you hit a dead-end. But if you do, there are some simple ways to get yourself back on track. It can help to put the thinking task to one side, switch off and go about your day-to-day activities.

This is because not all ideas are the product of hard work and intense concentration. In fact, some experts believe that ideas are like radio waves that float all around us waiting for us to tune into them. And when you alternate intense thinking with periods of rest, you often find that you open your antennae for flashes of inspiration. This usually happens when you're doing routine activities such as walking, running, washing up or taking a shower. These types of activities can increase alpha brainwaves (we'll look at this later, in Chapter 9). These put you in a relaxed enough state for your intuition to kick in, or for you to have an 'aha' moment.

It's also important to allow yourself to be bored and not to fill every moment with computer games, TV or Facebook updates. If you're prone to constantly keeping yourself busy, try to have 15 minutes a day where you do nothing. This could be as simple as just looking around you and letting your mind wander or listening to some music. You'll end up thinking in a much clearer, crisper way if you do this. Or course, if you're prone to endless day dreaming you may want to limit your free-form thinking time. But most people will find that regular creative boredom helps them organize their minds and their thinking.

It's also helpful to remember that being good at thinking isn't the same as being smart. In fact, some of the brainiest people are actually the worst thinkers because they often use their knowledge to defend a set way of thinking. Aim to be as open as possible when it comes to thinking about and discussing topics and ideas.

Transferring your skills to your degree

Remember that studies have shown that it's not the topics or issues you think about, but the fact that you learn and practise thinking skills techniques that is effective. So you can apply all these techniques to your university work with great effect.

It's also important to remember that whatever your thinking preferences, it's important that you think like 'you'. Your thinking is coloured by your perception. It is a sum of your education so far, your genes, your culture and your experiences. Just because you are now at university, you don't need to start thinking like a middle-aged, middle-class professor (unless that's indeed what you are!). Be confident enough to work towards whole-brain thinking that is resolutely you.

Further reading

Van den Brink-Bugden, R. (2010) *Advanced Critical Thinking Skills*. How To Books.

Student Comment

Ginny, Management Studies graduate

'I feel I am more inclined to think in a left-brain style and so when I force myself to think in a right-brain way, I feel bizarre. I can also feel overwhelmed when I have a whole topic in front of me as I don't know where to start. So I found having these thinking exercises really useful for when I feel blocked in this way. They enable you to focus on something other than your fears and, in the process, unblock.'

Greta says:

'It's important to keep pushing through despite these feelings by forcing yourself to think in these new strange ways. Just like in Chapter 4, if you throw yourself into these exercises, you will discover capabilities you didn't know you had. Your thinking processes will expand and you will simultaneously become more creative and analytical.'

Chapter 7

Powers of persuasion

Well thought out words are extremely powerful. In the past, history, folklore and the essence of culture were transmitted orally. And today, the spoken word has retained its power. From oaths and vows to political speeches, words can motivate and uplift or destroy and belittle. But the written word is especially persuasive because of its longevity – and the fact that you can carefully construct and reconstruct written arguments to have desired effects.

When you think of persuasive writing, it's likely that persuasive essays come to mind. But almost every piece of writing you do as a student needs to persuade in some way. From essays and dissertations to CVs and cover letters, your written documents need to convince readers to 'buy into' your point of view.

This chapter is about thinking persuasively and then turning those thoughts into persuasive words. So, if you're a little worn out from the thinking in the previous chapter, take a long, deep breath (or a mini 'mind' holiday), as you'll need to don your thinking cap once more for the exercises that follow.

Persuasive perspectives

To help you think (and write) persuasively, it helps to have some frameworks within which to consider the issues at hand. Here, I have identified 12 general perspectives in which you can frame your arguments. They are startlingly effective when combined as they demonstrate that you can approach a topic from a range of angles. This is useful because different perspectives will resonate with different people. So choosing a range of perspectives increases the chance that you will connect with more of your readers. When you actually come to writing persuasive essays, you don't need to use every single perspective and you can combine perspectives.

Here are the 12 perspectives to consider when creating persuasive arguments.

1. *Psychological*: look at the issue in terms of the thoughts, feelings and behaviours of the people involved.
2. *Cultural*: look at the issue in terms of the culture in which it's set. You could analyse what happens in different cultures and use that to relate back to the topic.
3. *Feminist*: look at the issue in terms of women and their place in society.
4. *Language*: look at the issue in terms of the language used to describe it. What associations do you have with the words? What do they mean or suggest to you? Are these the right words to use in the first place?
5. *Social*: look at the issue in terms of relationships or society's social structures.
6. *Financial/economic*: look at the issue in terms of money.
7. *Emotional*: look at the issue in terms of the emotions of the people involved.
8. *Factual*: look at the issue in terms of the facts.
9. *Family*: look at the issue in terms of the family of the people involved. You could also look at family structures in society as a whole.
10. *Historical*: look at the issue in terms of what has happened in the past – whether centuries ago or more recent.
11. *Scientific*: look at the issue in terms of science – this could be biology, chemistry, physics or another scientific discipline.
12. *Media*: look at the issue in terms of the media. Look at what TV, radio, newspapers, magazines or people in the public eye say about the issue.

To be persuasive, you also need to put yourself in your readers' shoes and empathize with how they are feeling. You can do this by stating what you believe to be their point of view, before you outline yours and back it up with both qualitative and quantitative evidence. Make sure that you don't just lay out impartial arguments. Your readers need to know your point of view and be persuaded to agree.

Exercise: Practising perspectives

Using each of the persuasive perspectives above, write out 12 arguments for the following question: 'Exams are a burden for students and should be scrapped. Argue either for or against.'

Your persuasive toolkit

Persuasive writing should include all of the elements below. So try to ensure that each persuasive document contains the entire toolkit.

1 *Credible content*: do background reading to get relevant, credible content. What are other academics saying about the issues? Gather together as many viewpoints as you can as this will help to spark your own creativity. If you're writing a personal essay or CV that can't be researched, you'll need to implement the thinking techniques from the previous chapter.
2 *Arguments*: carefully think through a series of logical arguments relating to your topic. For example: if iron cures anaemia and cockles are rich in iron, then cockles must cure anaemia.
3 *Counter arguments*: present the alternatives to these arguments. For instance, ask the questions, 'How many cockles would an anaemic person have to eat to be cured? Is this practical?'
4 *Qualitative evidence*: include descriptive examples that back-up your points. You might find an example of a cockle-eating anaemic.
5 *Quantitative evidence*: include facts, statistics and data. This could be the iron content of cockles and other related studies.
6 *Empathy*: finally, be attuned to what your reader needs and wants from your document and, if applicable, what their personal stance on the issue is likely to be. If it's an informal document, use the first- and second-person viewpoint to appeal directly to your readers. Make sure you use the audience tracker technique to give the readers what they want. Then structure all your arguments in terms of the things you think they are looking for.

It's not always easy to create arguments and counter-arguments – so at the end of the chapter I've recommended a clear, easy-to-read guide that will help you do so.

Exercise: Applying the persuasive toolkit

Using all the elements in the persuasive toolkit, take the question below and draw a mind map of the arguments.

'All students should be taught to think for themselves, instead of being made to adopt the beliefs of society. Argue either for or against.'

Then, write three paragraphs using the persuasive toolkit. Think of this as being a mini-essay, so revisit Chapter 3 and see if you can apply the openings and endings techniques to write an effective introduction and conclusion.

The important thing to remember in this exercise – and in persuasive writing in general – is to be holistic. Don't be afraid to put together converging perspectives. And use your imagination to create metaphors and other analogies that help you get your messages across. Keep using the techniques that you've learnt so far in this book. But decide whether you want to write in a formal or informal way, and revisit Chapter 5 to choose the techniques that will help you do so. If you choose to write informally, the words 'you', 'we', 'us' and 'our' are great for getting readers on your side.

Beyond persuasion

While it's important to write persuasively, it's also crucial to understand the differences between persuasive, descriptive and analytical writing – particularly when you come to write essays in the next chapter.

- **Persuasive writing** is writing that aims to bring the reader round to your point of view.
- **Descriptive writing** is writing that simply describes the issue.
- **Analytical writing** is writing that effectively argues all sides of an issue.

In many pieces of writing, you'll actually use a mixture of all three. Think of descriptive writing as answering the questions 'who?', 'what?', 'where?', 'when?' and 'how?' It's a step-by-step account of something that has happened. Analytical writing looks at this thing that has happened, takes a variety of perspectives and answers the question 'why?' Persuasive writing combines all these questions, putting forward a watertight case so that we believe there is only one plausible explanation. Imagine how a lawyer takes evidence and puts his or her own spin on it. However, an analyst instead presents the evidence and explains why it happened. At university level, you will never be asked to simply describe – there will always be some analysis or persuasion involved.

Exercise: Spotting persuasion

Which of the sentences below is persuasive, which is descriptive and which is analytical? Give reasons for your answers.

1 Approximately 800,000 people died in the genocide in Rwanda. These were predominantly people from the Tutsi ethnic group.
2 The genocide in Rwanda was entirely preventable.
3 Policymakers at the United Nations were aware that the Tutsi people were being targeted for elimination. However, there are many complex factors that account for their inaction in preventing the mass slaughter.

Answers

1 Descriptive – the sentences describe how many people were killed and which ethnic group they were from.
2 Persuasive – the sentence makes a bold assertion, with the aim of persuading the reader to believe this. In academic writing, this should be followed up with a reference to give credibility.
3 Analytical – the sentences begin to look in detail at the issues behind the genocide.

If your sole aim was to persuade, you would have example 2 as your main message. This would be the thing you distilled down to when doing the 'just one sentence' technique. And you would then ensure that all your description and analysis boiled down to focusing on this statement. Keep in mind that in essays and dissertations, you'll use a mixture of descriptive, persuasive and analytical writing. However, for other documents (as outlined in Chapters 11 and 12) you can afford to be bolder in your persuasion.

The techniques you've learnt here for creating persuasive arguments can be applied to anything you write. So don't save them only for when you're explicitly asked to persuade.

Further reading

Graff, G. and Biskenstein, C. (2010) *They Say, I Say: The Moves That Matter in Academic Writing*. Norton.

Student Comment

Emily, Pharmacy undergraduate

'I find it hard to compose personal pieces of writing where I have to give my own arguments, so it's great to have a framework of persuasion perspectives to work from. I'm good at writing descriptions, reports and analyses and so I know that I need to focus on creative and emotions-related language to write good cover letters and argumentative pieces.'

Greta says:

'Persuasion takes practice and if, like Emily, you feel that your work is not connecting emotionally to your readers then pay close attention to the verbs you're using. As we saw in Chapter 5, using verbs instead of nouns gives your work life and movement. But be sure to choose the most powerful ones you can. For example, verbs such as 'augment', 'administer', 'detect', 'bolster', 'generate', 'forecast' and 'influence' are powerful because they tell the reader to do something or show that something can be done. So, think about what verbs you use and whether you use them in the past or present tense. In Chapter 12, I call these verbs action words and explain how they're very effective when used in CVs.'

Part IV

Applying your knowledge

Chapter 8

Essay writing the easy way

Now that you've come this far, you should be familiar with the process for successfully writing documents. First, we laid the foundations in Part I. Then, in Part II, I outlined the first step, which is using your senses and creativity to generate impressions, metaphors, analogies and examples. The second step (in Part III) is applying integrated thinking, using a variety of techniques and perspectives. The third step (outlined here, in Part IV) is planning, organizing and producing clear and concise written work, using tried-and-tested techniques. So, this part of the book also aims to help you put all the previous steps into practice.

We'll begin with essays because if there's anything likely to strike terror into the heart of a student, it's the task of writing an essay. Just the mere mention can make you feel as though your lecturer has opened a trap door and is about to watch with glee as you fall to your doom.

University-level essays are certainly in a league of their own. Whether they're 2500 words, 5000 words or a relatively manageable 1500, they are likely to be considerably longer than you're used to. They also require intensive research. This is because your lecturers will never explicitly tell you what you need to include. It's up to you to do wider reading and then use your own judgement. And while you need to get most of your content from these sources, you can't copy anything. This means, to avoid plagiarism, you have to reference all your information, along with coming up with your own opinions and analysis. It's certainly an intense process.

So, I'll break it down by exploring the nuts and bolts of essay writing, giving you the practical tools you need. I'll also provide you with a step-by-step framework for putting together essays. However, it's still up to you to fill in the blanks with the techniques you've learnt so far.

So, what exactly is an essay?

First coined by sixteenth-century French writer Michel de Montaigne, the word essay is derived from the Latin word 'exagere', which means to weigh, sift and winnow. This is exactly what a good essay does. It weighs up ideas, sifts through arguments and winnows its way to a conclusion. Essays typically use formal techniques to do this, which is why they can often seem inaccessible. Many of the essays you've read may also contain convoluted language and lots of jargon. This can make the process of writing one seem all the more mystical. But it doesn't have to be this way.

Many people make the classic essay writing mistake of not directly answering the question. Instead, they fling all the knowledge they've gathered on the page, cross their fingers and hope that it demonstrates their understanding of the question. The trouble is that this way, the reader just feels bombarded without gaining any real insight. So remember that an essay is not a collection of facts or a culmination of everything you know about a particular topic. In fact, you may not even include everything you know, because you should only include the information that is relevant to the question. The essay question is the bullseye and your essay should be the dart that hits it. Granted, you may still get extra marks for hitting the areas around the bullseye but you will score highest if you keep targeting and hitting the bullseye.

How to interpret essay questions

Aside from fulfilling your course requirements, your main reasons for writing essays may be to inform, persuade, communicate, analyse, discover, prove a viewpoint or establish a cause and effect relationship between two or more things. The clue for what to do is in the question – but first you need to decipher it. Here is a list of the main key words in essays, along with an explanation of what each is asking you to do.

Account for: give reasons for and/or explain how something came about.

Analyse: examine the topic or argument in detail by breaking it down into parts and identifying the relationships between these parts.

Assess: decide how important the topic or argument is and give reasons for its value.

Comment on: Explain the importance of something.

Compare and contrast: describe and explore the similarities and differences between two things and comment on the significance of these.

Criticize: consider the evidence or arguments about something. Make a judgement about their merits and point out their faults.

Define: state precisely the meaning of something by doing a thorough exploration where you use examples.

Describe: give a detailed, critical account of what something is like.

Discuss: consider the arguments for and against something and then give your own opinion based on the evidence.

Distinguish: compare and contrast two things, showing you understand exactly what makes them different.

Elucidate: give a full explanation of something and make it crystal clear.

Evaluate: carefully look at the evidence about something and use this to make a judgement on it.

Examine: carefully look at something and explain the set of circumstances or reasoning that led to it. Then make a judgement on how valid it is.

Explain: give reasons for something using examples.

Outline: give a short description of the main points of something.

To what extent: discuss how accurate something is and present both sides of the argument.

The definitions above refer to the action part of essay questions, so they give you guidelines on what you have to do in a practical sense. But you still need to analyse all the other key words in a question (to find out what to do intellectually) and get information on how to approach the essay. Below is a three-step process you can follow every time you're set an essay question.

How to analyse essay questions

Step 1: Analyse the key words in the question

As an example, here's how you would analyse the following sociology question: 'Multiculturalism is a term that has outlived its usefulness, as it has become a catch-all word. Discuss.'

First, identify the key words in the question, these are:

- Multiculturalism
- Term
- Outlived
- Usefulness

- Catch-all
- Discuss

Then explore these words further by asking yourself questions such as:

- What exactly does multiculturalism mean? Does it mean different things to different people?
- What does the word 'term' mean? How useful are terms in themselves?
- The word 'outlived' suggests that multiculturalism is an old term. When was the term first coined and why? How has the term changed in the interim? What might be a better term now?
- How useful was the term in the past and how is it useful now?
- 'Catch-all' suggests that it is too broad – what are the pros and cons of having such a broad term?
- What are my discussion points both for and against the usefulness of the term?

Step 2: Look at your knowledge and identify what research you need to do

Do this by asking yourself questions such as:

- What gaps do I have in my knowledge?
- What do I most need to find out?
- How will I find this out?
- What sources can I use?

Step 3: Look at your goals for writing the essay

Do this by asking yourself questions such as:

- What am I aiming to do when I answer the question?
- Overall, what do I want to achieve through this essay?
- How do I want my readers to respond to my essay?

Exercise: Question analysis

Try the three-step process for yourself with the following question:

> Examine the statement: It is wrong for anyone to believe anything without sufficient evidence?

However, you don't need to answer your questions, save that for when you have a university essay to complete. Just brainstorm the questions you would ask yourself.

Organizing your information and ideas

If you follow the steps already laid out in this chapter, when you've been set an essay question, you'll generate plenty of quality content. Here are some tips for organizing that content.

Go colour crazy

Once you have all your information and ideas, grab a full spectrum of coloured pencils or pens and use different colours to group together the information and ideas that have things in common. Depending on the depth of your research, you could have 10–15 categories. Then write headings for each category, which should summarize your points or arguments.

Focus your message

Next, identify your main message. This is the standout point that you feel truly answers the question. If you're having trouble identifying your main message, do the 'just one sentence' technique learnt in Chapter 5. If you could answer the question in one sentence, what would you say?

Order, order

Now, decide on the order. The rule is to put the most important piece of information first, which should be your main message. Don't be afraid to answer the question outright and then discuss all the points in detail. This is much better than sending your readers on a treasure hunt, where they have to meander through wads of information before getting to the key points.

The building blocks of an essay

You now have a clear outline of your structure, so it's time to go one step further and break the content of your essay down into even smaller bite-size chunks, or building blocks, as I call them.

The best way to understand these blocks is to think of them in terms of being different types of information that can be combined together to create an essay. Don't think of these blocks as being nice neat bricks smoothly pasted together. Instead, think of them as being like crazy paving – haphazard arrangements of varying, jagged shapes that make an effective shape in the end. So, you can shift them around and (aside from the introduction and conclusion) use them in any order you like.

Using these building blocks can help you avoid putting in lots of citations and evidence without explaining why they're there or using them to answer the question. When you have to think about different types of information, it helps to switch on your evaluative brain. Using building blocks help to encourage you to weave your evidence and explanations throughout an essay, while exploring many different types of information.

Examples of building blocks

Below are examples of each building block taken from a variety of essays from different degree disciplines.

Introduction (uses a mixture of 'the story in a snapshot', 'a blast from the past' and 'the element of surprise' techniques)

Marcel Proust's 1.25 million word novel, *A la recherche du temps perdu*, is often said to be the greatest work of literature of the twentieth century. However, when first seeking publication, Proust was rejected by publishers and his work was criticized by friends. Yet, a century after the first part was published in 1913, his novel remains a renowned classic. When determining what exactly makes it a masterpiece, though, it is not easy to find a quick answer. In fact, it is difficult even to explain the contents of the book.

Analysis (weighing up arguments)

At first glance, the narrator's desire to possess may come across as a purely sexual desire. However, although he does not explain exactly what it is he hopes to possess, the use of the word 'savoir' suggests an intellectual desire.

Theory

The differential emotions theory suggests that when innate, prewired and packaged brain structures mature, they affect the relationships that people have with their environment.

Definition

Aristotle defines tragedy as being an imitation of actions of a certain magnitude – ones that are both serious and complete.

Anecdote (not suitable in all essays – ask your lecturer for guidance)

Amber was officially welcomed into her Ethiopian community at the age of 8, when her mother pinned her down and instructed a professional circumciser to slice off her genitalia. Battling through blurred vision, the elder tacked the remains with thorns, plucked from an acacia tree.

Facts and figures

According to the NHS, 36 per cent of pupils aged 11 to 15 have been offered drugs. By the time they are 15 years old, 18 per cent will be regular substance users (NHS 2012).

Point of view (this doesn't have to be your point of view)

Hobbes claims that if there is actually a possibility of proposing limits on the sovereign's authority, such proposals would always be open to judgement.

Statement

It is not possible to state objectively that Shakespeare and Milton are better writers than Hardy or Austen.

Description

Misconceptions are developed in order to understand the phenomena in the world. They often come from incorrect teaching at school, or from family and friends.

Quote (this is just one way to represent a quote; you can also use quote marks when copying sentences or short passages from other sources)

Santana said, 'I just dedicated every second of my life to training. I had to get used to life in England and the grass court.'

Example

In contrast, there were people in China, aside from the Red Guards, who disagreed with some of Mao's beliefs. For example, the author and playwright Jung Chang explains her experience of growing up during this period.

Conclusion (uses the 'round-up, round-up' technique)

The stunt reporters that emerged after Bly's asylum exposé rarely ventured from the standard and style she established. Her influence on the development of newspaperwomen is undeniable.

Exercise: Get scissor happy

To ensure that you are including as many of these building blocks as possible, or necessary, in your essays and effectively mixing and matching them, try the scissor happy technique. It's one that some journalists use when sifting through the information they've gained from interviews. Go through your colour-coded arguments/points, picking one at a time. Ensure these are printed or written on just one side of the paper and then take a pair of scissors and literally cut the paper into strips according to the building blocks. Organize your material in terms of information that is essential, important, nice-to-have and not important. Only keep the essential and important pieces of information and arrange these blocks in different orders until you find the sequence that's most effective, then sellotape them together. Use this as your master plan. Then, go back and see if any of the nice-to-have information adds something to this plan. If yes, include it. If no, bin it. And never include any unimportant information.

Writing your essay

There are three cornerstones to good essay writing: knowledge, expression and evaluation. Many students make the mistake of just applying knowledge and expression. They may write well and expressively but their work is solely descriptive. It simply presents the issues but doesn't evaluate them.

Knowledge: Doing background reading

In Chapter 3 you applied the active reading checklists in order to get information about how to write better. Now, apply the active reading checklists to help you interpret the information you've decided that you need to write your essay. Apply the 'plotting the arguments or narrative' exercise to ensure you have a good understanding of the material at hand.

Expression: Applying creative and writing techniques

Expression refers to the way you write about the essay questions. For most of your university essays, you will need to present an objective tone. Don't get thrown by the word 'tone'. It simply refers to your attitude about what you're writing about. To be objective, make sure you don't show any feelings for or against the topic. Just present, discuss and evaluate the topic. You can still present your points of view while being objective. Only use a subjective tone (one that is personal, emotional and biased) if you've been asked to write an informal, personal essay.

Before you even attempt to do any 'writing', you need to do some self-expression work (object writing and metaphors) to get your creative juices flowing. You can still do this, even if your final draft needs to be objective, because it warms up your writing muscles. Also, revisit Chapter 5 and apply tools from the all-purpose and formal toolkits to your essay.

Evaluation: Thinking and weighing up arguments

Evaluation makes a comment about something, either to criticize it, put it into context, or present the other side of the argument. Use the techniques learnt in Chapters 6 and 7 to create evaluative arguments. For example, ensure you draw a mind map of all the content you wish to include.

Introductions and conclusions

Use the openings and endings techniques outlined in Chapter 3 to help you write your introduction and conclusion. Make sure your introduction refers to the key statements in the question and throws up countless other questions or issues that you will answer or refer to in the main body of the essay. A good conclusion should not only sum up your main message but leave the readers feeling as though the essay has made some real progression from where it started.

Use paragraph power

Each paragraph needs to introduce a point and have a mini-conclusion. Some paragraphs will be directly connected and agree with the last, while others disagree and some totally change tack. But overall, there should be a through line, which is your main message or the theme of your essay. And each paragraph (and sometimes each point) should be joined to the last using the linking words learnt in Chapter 5.

Troubleshooting

When you're writing essays, you're bound to come up against some roadblocks. Here are six of the most common, along with remedies:

1 Lack of time

Estimate the amount of time you think it will take you to write your essay and then double or triple this as essays always take considerably longer to write than you think they will. As you've seen in this chapter, there are plenty of exercises to do before you begin the writing process. And even when you start writing, there's lots more thinking, planning and researching to do.

2 Boredom

If the essay question you've been set is incredibly dull, you need to find an angle into it that is interesting. Do additional research and speak to a librarian or lecturer in your department to find something that sparks off an interest. Then follow this track, weaving in all the necessary-but-dull information.

3 Getting caught up in definitions

When you're struggling to get your head around something, you can be tempted just to define it over and over again in different ways, using different quotes or different studies. But beware that by doing this you're not actually answering the question. Decide on one or two definitions that best suit you and then go back and follow the process outlined in this chapter. Remember, it's crucial to understand the key words in the question in plain, simple English before you go and research what experts and academics have said.

4 Not having enough information

You've done a good literature search and scoured journals for every possible source of information but you still don't have enough information to satisfy the word count. If you really can't find anything else to include, it's probably a sign that you haven't included enough discussion or evaluation in your essay. Avoid the temptation to pad your essays by writing long, winding sentences. This won't get you any additional marks and is bad practice.

5 Not knowing what's required of you

What is your lecturer looking for? What exactly do you need to do to get top marks? If you don't know the answers to these questions, it makes it doubly difficult to excel. So ask for guidelines and follow them as you're researching and writing, and review them afterwards. Remember, the rewriting, editing and proofreading phase is not just a cosmetic reading to pick up typos and spelling mistakes. It's also there to flag up possible issues, structural problems or, worse still, a crucial error or misunderstanding that will mean you have to do some serious backtracking or rewriting. This is one of the reasons why it's important to give yourself enough time.

6 Difficulty with referencing

You may be wondering where all the in-depth information is on referencing, but that is beyond the scope of this book. The aim of this chapter is for you to do the creative, analytic and narrative part of essays. Use this chapter to get this under your belt and see the further reading section of Chapter 5 for a resource on writing with sources.

Going for gold

It's true that the essay writing process can be gruelling and it can seem unfair that you have to spend so much time developing your writing skills when you're never actually directly graded on them. But the fact is that the content you choose and your writing skills *do* affect your essay grades. When you're judged by what you put on paper, it makes sense to make sure that it is as excellent as possible.

Further reading

Greetham, B. (2008) *How To Write Better Essays*. Palgrave.
Levin, P. ([2004] 2009) *Write Great Essays*. Open University Press.

Student Comment

Gail, Environmental Studies graduate

'The rules of essay writing that I was taught in high school completely block me, the minute I start writing. These are things such as, 'Don't use the word "I" in the first paragraph', and 'Always write five paragraphs in an essay.' It's as though I'm afraid of my old teacher's red pen if I break the rules.'

Greta says:

'Trying to write a university-level essay with the tools you learnt in high school is like trying to plan the design of a new town using GCSE-level Geography. It just doesn't work. There are so many basic essay writing rules that students learn in school. These include beginning paragraphs with the words 'firstly, secondly, thirdly . . .' and so on, making sure each paragraph has a 'topic sentence' and strictly adhering to the 'point, evidence, explanation' formula. The important thing is to remember that at university these rules are redundant. You need to throw them away. The only rules are that your essays need to be well researched, well thought-out and written in a way that fully discusses and analyses the ideas.'

Student Comment

Margaret, Economics undergraduate

'One of my writing types is Last-minute Lorraine, so I have problems in gathering my thoughts and putting them on the paper. This means I often postpone writing until the very end. When the deadline is near, I start writing and as a result of writing in haste and under time pressure the outcome seems ad-hoc, chaotic and missing many crucial points. To help solve this, I am going to buy a notebook and write down useful writing tips, phrases and formulations that will come in handy when writing essays that require expressing my own arguments.'

Greta says:

'Creating your own bespoke writing solutions to your problems is the ideal situation. So don't just think of this book as something that you passively follow. Be inspired by the student examples and the exercises and make the improvements that will most benefit you. If, like Margaret, you feel you could benefit from having some useful phrases to use in essays, the University of Manchester has created the *Academic Phrasebank* (www.phrasebank.manchester.ac.uk).'

Chapter 9

Writing in exams

Being able to perform under exam pressure is no mean feat. Exams can mean you have to focus intensely for up to three hours. For this reason, it's essential to not only master the writing skills techniques you have learnt so far, but to ensure you have sufficiently honed and perfected them so that you can deliver under pressure. This chapter is an exam writing boot camp where you'll complete a series of timed exercises.

Coursework versus exams

First, let's look at the differences between exam and coursework essays. In exams you have to take a series of shortcuts. This is because you have limited time and fewer words, so each word has to count. There is also no room for discussion that doesn't efficiently lead you to your chosen conclusion and directly answer the question. For coursework essays, it helps to think in terms of piecing together building blocks (as we saw in Chapter 8); however, in exam essays think in terms of arguments, discussion points or pieces of analysis. See Table 9.1 for a summary.

Exam question boot camp

The series of timed exercises (of 10 minutes, five minutes or 90 seconds) that follow require you to implement effective exam-style essay writing principles and choose which perspective you want to take on topics. So, with the 90-second bursts you don't have to write whole sentences (although of course, you can if you wish). This boot camp is about planning and as long as you understand your plan, you don't have to go into too much detail.

Table 9.1 Differences between coursework essays and exam essays

	Coursework essays	*Exam essays*
Analysing the question	Full, detailed analysis.	Highly condensed analysis.
Thinking	Explorative thinking on all the issues surrounding the question, including identifying what you don't know.	Condensed thinking that pieces together what you already know about the topics/issues.
Planning	Full, detailed process involving colour coding and carefully arranging information.	Snapshot decisions about which order your points should go in.
Writing	Contains fully fleshed-out introductions and conclusions. Things can be discussed in great detail with a keen eye for a good writing style.	Contains shorter, snappier introductions and conclusions. Cuts to the chase of what you want to say and uses a pragmatic style where the main focus is on answering the question in the allotted time.
Editing and proofreading	Can be fully revised several times and fully edited and proofread.	Can only be revised minimally with light editing; there is unlikely to be time for proofreading.

Take a past exam essay question of your choice and do the following timed exercises in order. Set a timer and ensure that you don't go over the allotted times. Do this whole series as a set and where there are two or more tasks listed in a particular time frame, spend the allotted time on *each* task.

In total, the workout below will take you 54.5 minutes if you do it exactly as prescribed. However, you should allow yourself 60 minutes to complete it. The remaining time is for breathing space, thinking and planning-on-the-go. In exams you need buffer room and so it's worth including this as part of your practice. Think of this boot camp as a highly detailed version of the process you'll undergo in an exam. When it comes to your exams, however, it's up to you to condense steps one, two, three and five, so that the majority of your time is spent writing.

Step 1: Analysing the question

Five minutes

1 Analyse the question in detail
2 Draw a mind map of the content you want to include

Step 2: Planning your content

90 seconds

1 Organize your ideas into categories
2 Choose your perspective and write your main message in one sentence
3 Decide which points are 'essential' and which are 'important'
4 Put your essential and important points in order

Step 3: Fleshing out your content

Five minutes

1 Write an introduction
2 Write down three studies, examples or points and identify how each answers the question

Step 4: Writing your content

10 minutes

1 Write three sets of arguments, counter-arguments, analysis or discussion (depending on the question)

Step 5: Ending, editing and proofreading

Five minutes

1 Write a conclusion
2 Proofread, edit and revise where necessary

After you've done this whole session repeat step 2 (points 2–4), ensuring that you choose a different perspective. Decide which one is your favourite perspective on the question. Is it the one you originally chose? If not, why not? Did you feel you rushed into choosing it because of time pressure the first time around?

In exams, you're forced to choose a perspective and doing this exercise means that you get to practise this in a safe setting. If you would have chosen differently, go back and explore how you would have answered the question using that perspective. Is it very different? Would your essay be any better for it? Understand that when you choose a perspective and wholeheartedly commit to it, you can score just as well as when you choose what you perceive to be a 'better' perspective but don't write such a good essay on it.

Here's an example of how my student Zenna answered part 4 of step 2. She used the social psychology question, 'The holocaust: why did it occur?'

- *Introduction*: defines and explains genocide.
- *Point 1*: anti-Semitism and the psychological needs behind it.
- *Point 2*: detailed analysis of in-groups and out-groups.
- *Point 3*: obedience theory and experiments to prove it.
- *Point 4*: the bystander effect.
- *Point 5*: group violence as a societal process.
- *Point 6*: the phases of the extermination process and how this links to in-groups and out-groups.
- *Point 7*: just world theory.
- *Point 8*: model of moral disengagement.
- *Point 9*: using the law as a justification for evil.
- *Conclusion*: summarizes the points above.

However, Zenna could have used a different perspective. She could have also put her points in the following order: 6, 5, 9, 3, 4, 2, 1, 7 and 8. Her introduction would have then been about genocide, putting it into the context of the extermination process that happened. The focus becomes different, which in effect makes it a very different essay.

Exam introductions and conclusions

Don't get too hung up on introductions and conclusions in exams. It's true that the introduction is the first thing the examiner will see, but in exams introductions are very different from the crafted kind you'll do in coursework essays. In fact, don't worry at all about being creative. Just focus on the key words in the question and what you intend to explore in the essay. The safest way is to begin with an interesting or surprising statement ('the element of surprise' technique) that cuts straight to the chase of what you want to discuss in the essay. Your conclusion can either use the 'round-up, round-up' technique or 'crystal ball gazing'. It's best not to use the 'from the horse's mouth' technique at the end as it can be difficult to end an exam essay effectively with a quote.

Planning in exams

Steps 1 and 2 of the exam boot camp are the planning steps you actually need to take in an exam. In a real exam situation, you need to spend around 10 minutes planning. You might think that it's foolhardy to spend precious minutes planning when you could be writing, but by doing so you will avoid many pitfalls. For example, my student Heema, studying undergraduate Economics says, 'In exams, I often find myself just repeating the same thing again and again because I have trouble putting my thoughts and ideas into words. I also find it difficult to write conclusions.' Heema is a Perfectionist Petra type who finds thinking and planning hard. Being repetitive is her way of trying to get things right but it doesn't work in exams. Heema needs to keep practising the exam boot camp and forcing herself to plan, until that planning behaviour becomes more and more natural.

But it's not enough to make a plan in an exam and then go merrily about your way, thinking that the job's been done. After you've finished each argument or point, you need to take stock and replan where you're going to go next. This way, if you feel you've gone a little off tangent in your last point, you can get yourself firmly back on the right road. Take control at every juncture of your essay. And don't be tempted just to write about what you *know*. Write about the issues in the question. If you haven't revised those issues or don't know much about them, you'll need to heavily analyse what you do know and plan in ways to link what you do know to the question at hand.

Getting in the zone

As you've seen, being able to analyse questions quickly, plan thoroughly, choose a perspective, think and plan on the go and keep your pen moving freely is a huge part of exam success. But a second crucial component is being able to put your mind and body in an ideal state to perform.

During exams how do you typically feel?

- Alert yet completely relaxed
- Frazzled and on edge
- Spaced out and sleepy

If you're like most people, you'll feel frazzled and on edge. When you're stressed, anxious or wired up on caffeine your brain responds accordingly by producing what are called beta brainwaves. Brainwaves are tiny oscillating electrical voltages in the brain and each wave is just a few millionths of a volt. But they can be responsible for how you feel, perform and respond. When you're operating from beta energy you'll feel productive and be able to work steadily, but you won't be able to have any spontaneous insights or inspiration. You may also feel anxious.

If you typically feel spaced out and sleepy during exams it's likely that you're operating from theta energy. When you're in this zone you'll feel especially dreamy and find it hard to access the get-up-and-go needed to perform at your best.

The optimum state to be in is to be alert and completely relaxed. When you feel this way, your brain is operating using alpha energy. When you're in the alpha state, all anxieties get washed away. You feel calm and creative and perform in a relaxed and effortless way.

Boosting alpha energy

Whether you're a member of your university hockey or rugby team, or prefer to get your exercise strolling to and from the student bar, raising your heart rate before writing is a great way to get in the zone. Yoga and meditation can also help to boost alpha energy – and even just taking a few deep breaths can be beneficial. Research by Ruvinsheteyn and Parrino found that listening to Baroque music while studying can help learning, thinking and creativity (Orel 2006). The effect is due to the fact that the music pulses at 60 beats per minute (BPM). To find out which of your favourite tracks are at the magic number 60, you can use analysing software such as *Mixmeister* or *Cadence*. Alternatively, do a Google search to find whole albums of music at 60 BPM. During the exam period when your thoughts are going haywire, you can ground yourself by walking barefoot on the grass and drinking calming drinks such as green and camomile tea.

Exercise: Five fun things to try

Taking inspiration from the suggestions above, brainstorm five specific ways that you can boost your alpha energy before and during exams.

1 ______________________________

____

2 ______________________________

____

3 ______________________________________

____

4 ______________________________________

____

____

5 ______________________________________

____

____

Finally, in this day of ubiquitous computers, iPods and iPads, make sure that you're actually familiar (and comfortable) with writing in longhand. So ensure that your exam preparation includes plenty of writing using a pen and paper. This will increase the likelihood of you physically being able to write as much as you can. It would be a shame to run out of time because your handwriting just wasn't up to par after too many hours at your computer.

Further reading

Cottrell, S. (2006) *The Exam Skills Handbook*. Palgrave.

Student Comment

Margaret, Economics undergraduate

'Perfectionist Petra is one of the writing types I identify with. I have always been like that as long as I can remember. My exam papers are always full of crossing outs and I frequently have to rewrite the entire exam paper because it's difficult to make out in the end. I know that getting better at writing will let me concentrate more on the content and consequently convey most of my knowledge about the subject. This focus will help me shift from nervously improving my exam paper in terms of its structure and using the time to expose my knowledge better.'

Greta says:

'It almost goes without saying that this is not helpful behaviour. Margaret needs to plan thoroughly in advance as this will help her to feel more confident during exams. She is wasting time in rewriting that could be spent expanding on points. She needs to give herself more time to think on the go, which will help solve this.'

Student Comment

Emily, Pharmacy undergraduate

'I feel so stressed when my writing is judged in exams. It's also so annoying that I sometimes have an idea but cannot seem to write it up on paper. And sometimes I cannot get simple things right I feel I should know.'

Greta says:

'After Emily got a deeper insight into her writing personality and the kinds of blocks she was facing (using Chapters 1 and 2) she was able to use the information to set herself some specific exam goals. She prepared for her exams by analysing pieces of writing (Chapter 3), doing object writing (Chapter 4) and applying thinking and expression techniques to her exam topics (Chapters 5 to 7). After going through this process she was much calmer when it came to exam time. "My ideas are flowing much more naturally now. I now feel that I can attempt my exams without feeling highly stressed", she said.'

Chapter 10

The write way to excellent dissertations

To thrive at university, you need to be a versatile writer. But even when you've successfully cut your teeth on a range of shorter documents, nothing quite mentally prepares you for the dissertation. At approximately 6000–20,000 words, dissertations are the longest document you'll have to write as an undergraduate. Not only that, you're free to choose a topic or hypothesis of your own, based on your interests. This freedom can be a bind, as it puts you – the student – firmly in the driving seat and makes you responsible for the success or failure of the avenue you choose to pursue. It's likely that you'll get help and support throughout most of the planning and research stages from your university. But when it comes to the writing, you're left alone with you, a heap of research and the blank page. So, here's a step-by-step guide to not only navigating the process, but writing an excellent dissertation along the way.

The big idea – finding your topic

When it comes to choosing your dissertation topic, it helps to set aside a considerable amount of time just for thinking. Use the techniques outlined in Chapter 6 and try not to settle on the first ideas that come to mind. Play with your ideas, be symbolic, use metaphors and even draw a metaphor table if you think it will help. Aim to go beyond the conventional way your degree topics are normally thought of.

Often the best ideas don't come until you've done an extensive thinking process. So, make way for your right-brain intuition to kick in by setting your initial ideas aside and following the advice in the 'Breaking through dead-ends' section in Chapter 6.

Exercise: Kick-starting your thinking

Here are some questions to help you get to that big idea.

What has been your favourite topic at university?

What issue in your degree has most interested you?

If you could change your degree discipline, what would you study?

If you weren't too embarrassed/afraid/daunted (delete or amend as appropriate) what would you love to write about?

What are you most curious about?

Make sure you answer these questions as quickly as possible, so that you don't second-guess yourself or over-think. It's important to listen to your first instincts. And don't worry if some of your answers seem completely unrelated to your degree. As you've seen in the 'persuasive perspectives' exercise in

Chapter 7, it's possible to marry ideas from a variety of disciplines. These questions are designed to kick-start your imagination, so feel free to ask yourself further questions that will help your ideas flow.

After completing this exercise, you should now have some leads to go on. But don't commit to any ideas or topics just yet as we still have more work to do. So, logically go through your papers, books, lecture notes and past essays to see what other topics resonate with you.

Exercise: Seven questions for your supervisor

Once you have some interesting ideas, it can help to go to your lecturer, tutor or project supervisor to discuss them before deciding on a final idea. You'll also need to know the form and function you're expected to follow in researching it. For instance, in Humanities and Arts degrees, a dissertation is most often a very long essay, separated into chapters. For other scientific and technical degrees, the dissertation is usually an extensive report or study (see Chapter 11 for more information). Be crystal clear in advance about what is expected of you. So ask the questions below and brainstorm some of your own to ensure you get every niggling worry answered.

1 What exactly is expected of me during the dissertation process?

____

____

2 How should I structure my dissertation?

____

____

3 How many words should I write in each section?

____

____

4 **How much original research should I do? How much of my research should be reviewing literature?**

____

____

5 **Do I need to do both qualitative and quantitative research?**

____

____

6 **Can I write in the first person for parts of the dissertation, or does the entire document need to be in the third person?**

____

____

7 **What do I need to do to get the best marks possible?**

____

____

Planning and preparation

With some care, attention and a sprinkling of luck, you should be well on your way to deciding on your final idea. You may have to write a proposal on it for your lecturer, tutor or project supervisor to sign off. If so, ensure that you include the following points:

- The main objectives of your research
- Your hypothesis (if it's scientific research)
- Theoretical reasons for choosing the topic
- The background reading that contributed to the ideas
- How you intend to conduct the research

- The resources and support you need
- The contribution your research will make to others

Even if you're not required to produce an official plan, it can help to write such a planning document for yourself to keep you on track.

Your writing is only as good as the quality of the reading you do, so your research has to be systematic, critical and have academic integrity. Choose your sources carefully and don't be afraid to ask for extra help from librarians, lecturers and other university staff. Also, revisit the planning techniques you learnt in Chapter 8 and use them to sort and organize your material.

Exercise: Finding your hooks

To keep you (and eventually your readers) interested, it helps to find hooks in your research. Put simply, a hook is something new, different or dramatic. Fiction writers use hooks all the time to keep you turning the page. For example, in a novel, the main character will suddenly black out just as the assassin is approaching, or the groom will run from the altar. Hooks create flow and can keep your dissertation alive and kicking.

To find your hooks, ask yourself the following three questions:

1. Which pieces of information are the most important?
2. What do I find highly unusual, interesting or surprising in my research?
3. What are my own conclusions or recommendations as a result of this?

You should use hooks at the beginning and end of each section. They ought to follow the same principles behind the techniques for introductions and conclusions that you learnt in Chapter 3. This means not including new information at the end of a section, but taking an interesting angle or slant on the information that enables the reader to see it in a new light.

For example, Theatre Studies student Grant opened the first chapter of his dissertation by stating that there is a little known history behind Chinese theatre. This tells the readers that they are going to learn something very new. He then opened Chapter 2 with a dramatic quote that outlined how the repercussions of theatrical 'model works' have left an indelible mark on Chinese culture today. This suggests that the reader is going to learn something about the wide and far-reaching consequences but we do not yet know whether these repercussions are positive or negative. He also used 'West meets East: Western productions in China' as a subtitle. This is a reversal of the more typically used 'East meets West' and so grabs the readers' attention. Finally, he used the literary technique of personification to end Chapter 2 in a powerful way, stating: 'China has finally grabbed freedom with both hands and will now power on to develop its theatre like never before.'

Bear in mind that your hooks need to form a consistent whole. So you need to decide what journey you want to take your reader on. Let the reader experience the uncertainty, varying viewpoints and brave new information that emerges through your research. And don't be afraid to make clear evaluative and recommendation points.

Crafting your title

Take time over crafting the title of your dissertation. You must include key words that summarize the main elements of the research. Prune out any extraneous words or phrases and make sure that your title doesn't give away your results. Apply the writing skills techniques learnt in Chapter 5. In particular, limit yourself to 15–20 words and ensure that, if you're writing the title in the form of a question, it's open. To do this, use the words 'who', 'what', 'where', 'when', 'why' or 'how' at the beginning so that the question can't be answered with a yes/no answer. These are general guidelines, so take note if your supervisor tells you otherwise. For example, some scientific disciplines advise not to phrase titles in question format.

Here are three examples of effective dissertation titles from my students:

- The effect of depression on perception and facial expression of emotions in adults
- How have the Chinese rebuilt their theatrical freedom since the Great Proletarian Cultural Revolution?
- What are the childcare needs of female business travellers?

Tackling the individual sections

The structure of your dissertation will vary, depending on your degree. Report-style dissertations will require an abstract (we'll look at this in the next chapter) and a section on research methods. Other dissertations will need an introduction, literature review, discussion and conclusion. Sometimes, there is just an introduction and conclusion with a series of chapters in between. The important thing is to ensure that you put into practice all the techniques you've learnt so far. In Chapter 13, there is a checklist of techniques that you can refer to, in order to help ensure that your dissertation ticks all the boxes.

Breaking writer's block

If you're still having trouble getting pen to paper (or fingers to keyboard), these tips can help:

- Write for just 10 minutes a day; no more, no less. Do this for several days until you actually start to feel energized to write more. Then, increase the time you write by 15- or 20-minute increments until you're putting in sessions of up to two hours.
- Get up and go straight to your desk before you've even had breakfast or brushed your teeth – and just write. This can help you bypass your critical left brain that in your half-awakened state shouldn't be switched on yet.
- Do three pages of free writing before tackling your dissertation. To do this, just write anything that comes into your head. The only rule is that you have to keep your pen moving. If you can't think of anything to write, then literally write, 'I have nothing to write.' The physical act of writing anything can help to free you up to complete the task at hand.

The hero's journey

Your experience of writing a dissertation can feel like an epic battle. A helpful way to tackle it is to use the concept of the 'hero's journey'. This is a term coined by Joseph Campbell (1949) to describe a basic pattern found in stories across the world. The hero responds to a 'call to adventure' before embarking on a major transformation, which he or she then shares with the world. It's true that your dissertation is unlikely to shape humanity as we know it, but it can help to think of your hero's journey in terms of a series of trials and tribulations that will change you. For example, you may go down one research path and it doesn't work out; you choose another and then fight to get the permissions needed. Perhaps the data gets skewed, your literature review isn't initially up to scratch or you simply don't find what you need. The point is that if you look upon it as a hero's journey, you'll be better prepared for the ups and downs that inevitably come with it. So, think of your dissertation in these terms and plan in advance extra time to go through some hardships.

Keeping calm

If you're feeling overwhelmed, temporarily stop your research as there's no point creating even further information overload. You may actually be doing too much research and that can cause a blank mind as you struggle to make sense of too much information. Go back to basics and look at your original proposal and ideas and write in simple language about them. Stop reading for now, and instead just write everything you know about your research. You can always go back to your books and journals once you're feeling calmer.

If even that doesn't work, then step away from the computer and get grounded. See Chapter 9 for tips on raising your alpha energy and follow them to try to get back in the zone.

Further reading

Swetnam, D. and Swetnam, R. (2009) *Writing Your Dissertation*, 3rd edn. How to Books.

Student Comment

Zenna, Psychology undergraduate

'I find big writing assignments and dissertations very hard to do. Having a blank mind or having no idea how to write a piece is very frustrating. Also, not being able to organize the paragraphs in correct and flawless order is very exhausting.'

Greta says:

'You're obviously feeling that your work doesn't flow and appears to be a collection of disjointed paragraphs. You're probably feeling this way because you don't have a clear enough main message that acts as a 'through-line' throughout your dissertation. In this case you have to go back to the drawing board or the 'thinking board', as it were, and decide exactly what you want to say. When your thoughts are clear you can get rid of the type of panic behaviour that causes you to sit at the computer and endlessly cut and paste and rearrange and feel that you are ending up with a bigger and bigger mess. So, put your books, research papers and dissertation aside and take a pad of paper and pencil and write down in simple English your main message or messages and how they link all the information together. If you find this really difficult to do then there are clearly gaps in your knowledge and this can be at the root of the problem. Fix this and it will help your work to flow.'

Chapter 11

Apply your skills to other documents

In your degree it's what you put in writing that counts. Even in degrees such as Performing Arts, the emphasis is less on your ability to orate Shakespeare than your ability to put in writing the tools and techniques for doing so. You also need to produce a repertoire of documents, meaning your experience needs to go beyond the essays and dissertations we've looked at so far. So we're going to continue in the practical vein of Part IV with tools, techniques and advice for applying your skills to articles, reports and speeches.

WRITING ARTICLES

Like essays, the purpose of articles may be to inform, persuade, communicate, analyse, discover, prove a viewpoint or establish a cause and effect relationship between two or more things. But, crucially, articles must also entertain. However, the tone is often subjective and the language more informal. The facts are often viewed through the lens of the writer's opinions and even political stance. Articles can be effective documents because they provide a snapshot into topics. For instance, an article could summarize a book, take a stance on a controversial issue or be a thought-provoking call to action. They are very versatile and their length (usually 500–2500 words) makes them accessible for readers.

The types of articles we'll look at in this chapter are not the sort that PhD types write for peer-reviewed journals. These articles always include citations and footnotes and follow a strict essay-style format. Instead, we'll look at a more user-friendly style of article that could belong in a trade magazine, for instance. Trade magazines are linked to professions, and include titles such as *Nursing Times, Accounting Age* and *Pharmaceutical Field.* In these types of magazines, the language used is more simple, direct and easy to digest.

Unless you're studying journalism or media, it's unlikely that you'll have to write articles as a mandatory part of your course. But learning the skills means that you can contribute articles to your university magazine or newspaper. The ability to write articles is also a good skill to have in your future professional life, as publishing articles is an excellent way of positioning yourself as an expert in your field.

Your mission (should you choose to accept it)

The easiest way to show you how to write an article is to set you a challenge to write one and then outline the different elements that go into the writing process. So your goal is to write an article about the benefits of eating five pieces of fruit and vegetables a day. I have chosen this topic because it is neutral and can be looked at from any of the persuasive perspectives outlined in Chapter 7. For instance, if you're studying tourism, you can look at how we're eating far more imported fruits than ever and getting a taste for tropical varieties when travelling abroad. Or if you're studying English Literature, you could compare real and fictional examples of people who don't get their 'five a day'.

Step 1: Understand your readers

Pick a group of readers you want to write for and then complete the audience tracker technique from Chapter 5. Also, ask yourself additional questions that may help you to write for your readers. For instance, ask:

- What hobbies do my readers have?
- If I sat down with my readers, what would we talk about?
- What are my readers' main problems?
- How will this information affect the examples or language that I'll use in the article?

Step 2: Do your research

Here's a rundown of the types of research you'll need:

- Interviews
- Facts and figures
- Arguments for
- Arguments against

- First person opinions
- Real-life examples

Before you begin to research your own article, it's helpful to get an insight into the type of research that professional journalists do. Gather together three very different magazines. Choose an article from each magazine and note down examples of the types of research using the headings above. With regard to interviews, also note down who they're with and what they're about.

Where to find your own research

Look in books, magazines and on the internet for information. The first person opinions and real-life examples can be your own or those of others'. To find other people's views, read interviews and opinion pieces, or conduct your own interviews.

Conducting insightful interviews

Use the tips below to prepare and deliver effective interviews:

- Use your research to help you prepare a list of questions in advance, so that you have a rough idea of where you want the interview to go. However, be open to new information and leads. Make sure you use open questions beginning with 'who', 'what', 'where', 'when', 'why' and 'how'.
- Create rapport and put your interviewee at ease. You can 'break the ice' by making a statement about the weather, giving a compliment (one that's not too personal) or asking an interesting question about an unrelated topic that you think your interviewee will be interested in.
- Make use of prompts and refer back to previous comments in the interview to find out more. Use phrases such as, 'So when you said . . .?' and 'Going back to . . .?' Aim to be as curious as possible and keep your interviewee on track so that you get the information you need.
- If your interviewee is closed-off and not giving you much information, make your questions more specific. For instance, instead of saying, 'What are the best fruit and vegetables to eat?' ask, 'Which has more nutritional value, mangos or apples?' By being specific, you then force your interviewee to start giving specific answers.
- Make sure you have all the factual information you need to write the article. This includes the full name and correct spelling of the people you've interviewed and any key dates, events and other facts you want to include.

Also, make sure you have your interviewee's contact details in case you want to get back in touch to clarify anything.

- If you're interviewing someone official, or even a celebrity, it's best to use a Dictaphone to make sure that your quotes are 100 per cent accurate. For most other interviews, it's fine to write down everything in longhand (as fast as you can!).
- Try to interview more than one person (and more than one type of person) to get a range of views. For example, if you were writing an article for parents, you could interview a government official, a primary school teacher and a single mother on a tight budget.

The building blocks of articles

In Chapter 8, we looked at essays consisting of the following building blocks:

- Introduction
- Analysis (weighing up arguments)
- Theory
- Definition
- Anecdote
- Facts and figures
- Point of view
- Statement
- Description
- Quote
- Example
- Conclusion

The good news is that you can use all of these in articles – just be careful about including too much theory. Examples and real-life stories are much more effective. The introductions and conclusions are the same as we've looked at in previous chapters.

However, there are some additional building blocks that can be used in articles (I'll expand on each one in more detail below):

- Headline
- Standfirst

- Analogy
- Question
- Advice

The techniques behind good headlines

The headline is one of the most important parts of an article. If it doesn't grab the readers' attention, they are unlikely to read on. So, good headlines need to be emotive. They ought to address a problem your readers have, or an issue that they're interested in, while also being a summary of what the article is about.

Most headlines fall into one of the following categories:

Question: Are you a clutter junkie?

Quote: 'I was a teen beauty queen'

Pun: A thirst for learning: how water transformed one school

Alliteration: The fight for freedom

Exclamation: Education, education, education!

> **Exercise: Spotting headlines**
>
> **Flick through some magazines and see if you can find examples of each of the headlines above. Note that some writers use more than one technique at once, which makes their headlines doubly or triply powerful.**

Standout standfirsts

As the name suggests, the standfirst is the first part of the article that introduces what the article is about and often introduces the writer too. It is usually only two or three sentences long. For example: 'Being clutter free can help you to be carefree. It's time to de-junk, says Greta Solomon.'

Notice that this standfirst also uses alliteration and a repetition of the word 'free'.

Amazing analogies

An analogy is a comparison of the similarities between two things which are otherwise unlike one another. If you use examples that your readers will understand and relate to, it can help to get your points across. You can be creative with analogies and use metaphor tables to help you think them up. For example, 'Having a house teeming with items is like trying to swim in a pool full of life rafts. The rafts may make you feel safe and secure but they slow you down and hinder your progress.'

Quick questions

Asking questions is effective in articles, as it enables you to speak directly to your readers. For example: 'Do you have a clutter problem?'

Active advice

Not all articles give advice, but it is essential if you want to show your readers how to do something. For example: 'Spend 15 minutes a day tackling clutter that is easy to throw away, donate to charity, sell or recycle. Finally, each time you go shopping ask yourself: do I really need this?'

Exercise: Spotting article building blocks

Use the article below and annotate it, marking all the different building blocks. See if you can also spot the types of introduction and conclusion, creative and literary techniques that have been used. After you have finished making your notes, write a short paragraph that sums up why you think this is a good article. Use this article as inspiration for your own article on fruit and vegetables.

Go green or guzzle gas?

With oil prices crashing – does anyone still care about environmentally friendly vehicles? Greta Solomon finds out

There was a time when hybrid cars, combining electricity with petrol, were the glowing beacon of the future. The world was using too much oil and consumers needed to take action. Energy-efficient motoring seemed to be the answer to the world's woes. Then came the global economic meltdown and with it a worldwide drop in the demand for oil. This caused petrol prices to plummet to what the Automobile Association (AA) calls a three-year low. The recession also heralded a change in consumer buying behaviour. New cars no longer flew off the forecourts and people became cautious spenders.

When prices were high, it seemed that car drivers seriously looked at the way they were consuming the world's natural resources. Initial evidence suggested that consumers were opting for more fuel-efficient cars. Despite being expensive to buy, the savings made sense. The Toyota Prius, for instance, has a list price of over £17,000. But when petrol prices were high, drivers could still save money on a per-mile basis. Now that petrol prices have crashed, driving a hybrid vehicle can be more expensive than a less fuel-efficient car.

The current economic climate is one where people struggle to get cheap credit and live in fear of redundancy. The average consumer is likely to opt for a cost-efficient runaround, even if it is at the expense of the environment. Historically, demand for petrol has been inelastic. No matter the price, we still fill up, through gritted teeth if necessary. We're addicted to the hooch and will get it at almost any price. When prices were high, hybrid vehicles were a socially acceptable way to justify spending vast amounts of money on this addiction.

However, the psychology of buying comes down to more than just pennies and pounds. We also buy to make ourselves feel good; to feel like we're one step ahead of the pack; to bolster our image. Buying a fashionable, environmentally friendly vehicle in a buoyant economy is a great idea. We can whack it on a cheap finance deal and simultaneously save at the petrol pumps. But low petrol prices simply provide little incentive to go green. The only immediate benefit is the ego boost of having done a worthy deed – a lustre that soon fades.

That's not to say that there will be a total demise of the environmentally friendly vehicle. The British government has still made a landmark European Union deal to cut tailpipe emissions by 18 per cent. However, they've pushed the deadline from 2012 to 2015 to give car manufacturers a little longer to keep creating fuel monsters. If there's currently less demand for green vehicles (and vehicles overall) it makes sense for car manufacturers to wait until they flood the market with them.

However, it seems that this is all just a hiatus before oil prices inevitably shoot up again. Then we'll throw our hands up in dismay at how wasteful we're being to the environment with our gas-guzzling cars. Until the cost of petrol really hits our wallets too hard, we'll keep filling up and driving on, whether or not our cars are environmentally friendly.

Step 3: Plan like a professional

Use the same planning and structuring methods outlined in Chapter 8, and decide on your main message. Also make sure you apply all the thinking and brainstorming techniques you've learnt in this book so far. In addition, do 10 minutes of object writing on 'fruit and vegetables' and underline the words and phrases you think would be excellent for your article.

Step 4: Decide on your tone

Decide whether you want your article to be serious, humorous, educational, ironic, or something else entirely.

Step 5: Tackle the key building blocks first

Write your headline, introduction and conclusion first so that you know exactly where you're going with your article. Spend time getting these building blocks right and the rest of your article will flow.

Mission accomplished

Now you have all the building blocks for your article, you need to put it all together. But here are some other things to bear in mind. The first thing is to make sure that you put each paragraph in context. You need to convince your readers that what you're writing about makes logical sense, so don't be afraid to explain yourself and keep backing yourself up with facts, statistics, quotes and examples.

Remember that articles should be entertaining, so include lively analogies and metaphors. Don't be afraid to speak directly to your readers using the first-person and second-person viewpoints. Finally, you should write approximately 1500 words.

WRITING REPORTS

Before we get going with report writing, it's important to note that if your dissertation needs to be written in report format, then you should use this section in conjunction with the previous chapter.

The purpose of a report is to analyse or investigate a topic and make clear recommendations about it. Reports are formal documents, so they use formal language and take an objective tone. And any recommendations you make in a report should arise from the facts presented. Reports usually follow set headings. These vary, but generally speaking they are:

- Abstract
- Introduction
- Main body
- Results (if it's a scientific report)
- Discussion
- Conclusion

Writing an effective abstract

An abstract is like a bite-size report, so its structure should follow the structure of your report. Its purpose is to give your readers an overview of the main points in your report, and entice them to want to read more. So it should begin with an outline of the problems or issues you discuss; state the purpose of the report; give brief details about the approach or methods used, and present the key findings and conclusions. The structure of the abstract follows the structure of the report. If your dissertation is in report format, you'll almost certainly need to write an abstract. If so, tackle it last when you have an overview of your entire report, have fully analysed your findings and come to clear conclusions.

What *not* to do

Ensure that your abstract doesn't read like a list of contents in prose form. Similarly, avoid making your abstract a summary of everything that the report intends to do. So don't write: 'This report will consider the political events which occurred during the Great Cultural Revolution in China and the freedom that Chinese theatres have today.' Instead, present the key findings. For example, describe what political events happened, how this impacted on the Chinese theatre and what the new freedom looks like. Abstracts can be as short as 150–200 words (however, check with your lecturer about your word limit). So don't meet the word count by leaving out information. It's better to write too much and then go through and do a ruthless edit.

What you *ought* to do

As a model of what to do, here is an example of a good science abstract, written by Psychology student Irina. Here, she has summarized everything in her report.

> Research has shown that differences in the moral reasoning maturity of offenders affects the nature of the offences they commit. The authors used

a structured postal survey to examine differences in personality and socio-moral reasoning between violent (n=9) and non-violent (n=7) groups of adult offenders. An analysis of Covariance (Ancova) on the socio-moral reasoning scores with socio-economic status, chronological age and verbal intelligence as covariates was conducted. It indicated no significant difference in the global stages of socio-moral reasoning between the two groups of offenders. The majority of offenders were reasoning at the conventional level. However, there was a significant difference between the two samples when comparing the five moral values of contract and truth, affiliation, life, property and law and legal justice. Violent offenders scored significantly higher on the life value compared to the other moral values.

Learning the process behind writing a good abstract can actually help you to write your entire report. This is because it requires you to condense your points, arguments and findings into one or two paragraphs.

Turning your article into a report

Reports need to have a formal, objective tone which is very different from articles. So, it's likely that you'll have to adapt the informal, subjective language you used in your article. You don't need to rewrite your entire article though, as it's unlikely that you'll ever have to turn an article into a report at university. This is just for practice purposes. So, below, we'll just practise a couple of skills that will demonstrate some differences between articles and reports. First, we'll look at the language.

Exercise: Making the informal, formal

Identify some informal phrases from your 'fruit and vegetables' article and write their formal equivalents. To help you practise this, below are some informal phrases from the 'oil prices' article. See if you can find the formal alternatives for these phrases.

Glowing beacon of the future

____

____

The world's woes

____

____

This caused petrol prices to plummet

____

____

New cars flew off the forecourts

____

____

The average customer is likely to opt for a cost-efficient runaround

____

____

We're addicted to the hooch

____

____

The psychology of buying is about more than just pennies and pounds

____

____

We can whack it on a cheap finance deal

____

____

Fuel monsters

____

____

Gas-guzzling cars

____

____

Exercise: Planning your sections

Next, draw a plan that compares the differences between your article and report. Use the headings: 'Readers', 'Main message', 'Headline', 'Introduction' and 'Conclusion' and draw and fill in your own table, using the same format as Table 11.1.

Next, decide what information should go in which section of *your* report, using the report headings outlined at the beginning of the chapter. Then, once you've done this, write an abstract.

TURNING YOUR ARTICLE INTO A SPEECH

It's written in folklore that the average (sane) human being would rather die than speak in public. So it's not surprising that those who can speak up for themselves get ahead. But before you deliver a speech, you need to write it. As you've no doubt guessed, the process for preparing to write a speech and the techniques used are similar to those for writing an article. With regard to language and tone, speeches are much like articles.

Here are seven tips to help you write a speech:

1 Introduce yourself at the beginning of the speech, explain your credentials for giving the speech and tell the listeners what you will talk about.

Table 11.1 Turning the article about oil prices and environmentally friendly vehicles into a report

	Article	*Report*
Readers	The general public aged 18–60 who would read the environment pages of a local or national newspaper.	Manufacturers of hybrid vehicles.
Main message	Oil prices are in flux and so is consumer behaviour, but ultimately all consumers really care about is the cost of motoring.	Recommend that a public relations campaign is launched to persuade people to keep buying hybrid vehicles despite crashing oil prices and the recession.
Headline	Go green or guzzle gas?	Persuading the public to buy hybrid vehicles.
Introduction	There was a time when hybrid cars, combining electricity with petrol, were the glowing beacon of the future. The world was using too much oil and consumers needed to take action.	Evidence shows that consumers want to buy environmentally friendly vehicles.
Conclusion	Until the cost of petrol really hits our wallets too hard, we'll keep filling up and driving on, whether or not our cars are environmentally friendly.	It's essential to crystallize the five good reasons why consumers should buy these vehicles. Having each reason promoted by a celebrity that reaches a certain segment of the demographics that buy these cars can help to encourage consumers to make the choice to buy a hybrid vehicle.

2 Create a framework for your speech. This can be three steps to doing something, or you can use a metaphor to describe the thing you're talking about. For example, if you were talking about something that had two halves to it, you could use the metaphor of a football game and explain everything in terms of the players, the ball and the referee. Be creative and find a structure that works for you.

3 Make good use of metaphors, literary techniques and analogies. Create stories and paint vivid word pictures to make the content come alive for the listeners.

4 Use active and simple language throughout, sticking to the first and second person. Remember, your listeners will easily tire if the sentences are too complicated.

5 Keep your sentences short – you should be able to read an entire sentence in one comfortable breath.

6 Make the end of the speech in some way link back to the beginning and finish with the power of three, if possible. Remember to thank the audience for coming.

7 Once you're finished with the writing process, make sure that reading aloud is part of your editing process. If anything doesn't sound right, revise it.

Exercise: A final speech

Now, your task is to adapt the information from your article into a short three-minute speech that you can deliver to any willing audience, even if it's your pet goldfish!

By now, you should be starting to see that once you have a base of good writing skills, they can 'cross over' to a variety of documents. But at heart, it's essential to understand what exactly is required of you with every document you need to write. So, if in doubt: ask. And then keep asking until you're crystal clear about what you have to do. This will give you a fighting chance of choosing the right tools and techniques from this book to enable you to write clear, concise and effective documents.

Further reading

Bowden, J. ([2009] 2011) *Writing a Report.* How To Books.

Student Comment

Grant, Theatre Studies undergraduate

'I finally have a method for writing articles and reports – it's made the whole process so much simpler!'

Greta says:

'So much of writing can be broken down into steps and processes, which leaves you free to concentrate on what you want to say, and how you want to say it. The more techniques you master, the easier your writing becomes.'

Chapter 12

Navigate the road ahead

There are some degrees, such as Nursing, Public Relations and Accounting, that prepare you directly for the world of work. But most university courses are simply not vocational. And even when they are, there is no guarantee of a job after graduation. When the 2008 recession hit, graduate unemployment sharply increased. Now, it remains high and looks set to stay that way. In fact, one in every five new graduates is unemployed (Office for National Statistics 2012).

However, take heart, as this chapter isn't about getting caught up in the doom and gloom of recessions. Yes, there are former bankers living out of their suitcases and hundreds of graduates applying for minimum wage jobs. But if you look at the bigger picture, you'll see that all is not as it seems. The shift in the job situation is not solely down to the recession. The internet is now king and it continues to change the face of work. Many jobs that existed twenty years ago have simply died out. New industries are emerging, which are full of opportunities. However, in our new 'social networked' world, these new jobs increasingly require you to be innovative, use specialized knowledge and skills and have the ability to connect well with others.

Building your personal brand

So, what does this all mean for you, as a university student or graduate? Well, it means you may have to disregard the conventional wisdom about job hunting and career choice because the work landscape will continue to flux and shift. There is no longer a neat through line between a good education and a good job. Experts estimate that the average graduate could have 15–20 jobs in his or her lifetime – in more than one career. So, it means that you need to create your own set of stepping stones to bridge the gap between your degree and your ultimate ambitions. To borrow a well-worn business cliché, you need to 'think out of the box'.

In fact, if you Google university graduation speeches, you'll see that the world's leading movers and shakers don't recommend that you choose a nice, safe job in a good company but be inspired and take a few bold risks. By doing so, you give yourself a chance of becoming the type of person that everyone wants to employ – irrespective of industry or subject speciality.

But if you'd like to remain firmly 'in the box' and can't see yourself trailblazing new paths, then there are still excellent corporate jobs available for the right candidates. But it'll take far more than a good degree to land them.

Honing your soft skills

Qualifications alone don't sell themselves any more, so you need to see yourself as a package, not as a vessel for your degree. So, if you want to make the most of your degree after graduation, you have to hone your 'soft skills'. Think of these as being desirable personality traits. For example, employers want to hire people who are creative, resourceful and resilient. But the amazing thing is that – despite high unemployment – many say they cannot find them!

Taking engineering employers as a case in point, a report by Ardington (2011) states that they want the seven Cs in graduates: common sense, creativity, communication, collaboration (teamwork), commitment (project management), command (leadership) and caring (interpersonal skills). And this list isn't exclusive to engineering – it can be applied to virtually any job.

The good news is that this book has been a whole course in soft skills. It has aimed to increase emotional intelligence, thinking ability and your ability to communicate effectively with yourself and others – skills you need both at university and beyond. And, of course, it's tackled writing skills.

In this chapter, I'll present a step-by-step guide to writing personal statements, CVs, cover letters and other 'selling' documents that will help you land your dream job – even if this 'job' is actually starting your own business, or landing an interim placement before you go onto further study. Whatever it is you choose to do, the first step is being able to write your personal story effectively.

What's your story?

The first step is to draw a mind map of all your personal skills and qualities. Think about the personal qualities outlined in Chapter 2, and include absolutely everything that you can think of. Ask yourself, 'What trials and tribulations have I gone through that have changed me for the better, or led to success?'

The next step is to put these skills and personal qualities into a framework. In his book *The Seven Basic Plots*, Christopher Booker has stated that there are only seven basic stories in the world (Booker 2005). Granted, the characters and details change, but each story follows one of seven well-worn trajectories. Organizing your skills and personal qualities into stories can help you to put an interesting spin on your life, educational and work history. They also help you to talk more eloquently about yourself in interviews and can help you explain seemingly incongruous facts or events in your education or work history.

Out of the seven, there are five stories that are likely to be most relevant to your life. These are:

- *Rags to riches:* the story of a poor person who overcomes the odds to be rich. The riches don't have to be monetary; they can be something great that was attained from virtually nothing.
- *The quest:* the story of someone's long, difficult journey towards a distant, yet vital goal. Sometimes, the journey becomes as important as the destination.
- *Voyage and return:* the story of someone whose journey takes them right back to where they started.
- *Triumph over tragedy:* the story of someone who enters a 'dark place' yet overcomes the challenges they face in a life-altering way.
- *Rebirth:* the story of someone who falls into a literal or symbolic death state before being reborn and 'coming back to life'.

Exercise: Writing your personal stories

Take each story and write an example of it from your life, education and work. Think of these stories as being like the 'story in a snapshot' introductions we first looked at in Chapter 3. So, ensure each story is no longer than a paragraph or two. Next, pick your favourite story out of these and craft it into a finished piece of prose by rewriting, editing and proofreading it. Make sure your story is written in the first person and is themed around achievement, status, responsibility, reputation, personal growth or fulfilment. You can use a version of this story in a personal statement or cover letter, if appropriate.

Here is an example of a 'triumph over tragedy' story from Economics undergraduate, Margaret.

Triumph over tragedy

I was once rejected when applying for a top London university. I felt so hurt that I decided to travel there to ask for the reason for my rejection. As it could be predicted, I didn't get any concrete answers. Unfortunately, the trip cost me a lot and I ran out of money to buy a return ticket to Glasgow. I decided to hitchhike. I met many people on my way back and the conversations I had with them influenced my life. In many ways this trip itself was invaluable to me. A year later, I met my future husband. Two years later I was accepted at another university.

Modelling an effective personal statement

In its traditional sense, a personal statement is a 500- to 600-word document that you use to help persuade admissions tutors to admit you into a university course. But learning to write a good personal statement can help you develop the skills to write effective cover letters, and can even help you when filling in job application forms.

Below is an example of a personal statement that my student Faheela used to secure a place on a Master's degree course in Chemistry.

Faheela's personal statement

'In medicinal chemistry, the chemist attempts to design and synthesize a medicine or a pharmaceutical agent which will benefit humanity', says organic chemist, Graham Patrick. It is my goal to become a medicinal chemist and explore the links between disease, mechanisms of action and the development of safe, effective, commercial drugs. Chemistry is the science that shapes the world we will live in tomorrow.

I feel that I am a natural-born chemist and I am never happier than when experimenting; whether in the kitchen while cooking or in the laboratory. However, during my degree I became fascinated by organic chemistry, in particular cancer chemotherapy and medicinal chemistry. Chemistry has the power to improve the quality of life by manipulating the structures of substances for medicinal purposes. For instance, currently, Taxol (extracted from the Pacific yew tree bark) is a popular anti-cancer agent. However, it takes a hundred years to grow one tree to make just 300mg of Taxol – so this is not a sustainable source.

I would love to be able to tackle complex drug design in the future. My final year project, 'Protecting groups for amines', where I researched over 40 journals, taught me about protecting reactive functional groups, and this has inspired me further.

Through undertaking advanced experiments, I have developed patience, creativity in using journals to research procedures, persistence when I don't instantly get the right results, the maturity to deal with harmful chemicals and the diligence needed to remain safe at all times. I have achieved mostly As across my reports and learnt how to produce extensive written projects.

Therefore, my ultimate goal is to be a researcher in the field of medicinal chemistry. I am choosing the Masters route because I want to ensure that I gain the best knowledge and laboratory skills possible and to ensure that my knowledge is fully fleshed out and complete. This will be vital when I embark on PhD studies in the future.

I am a motivator and I would love to enhance other people's lives through chemistry. My passion for education has also been shown through my work as head teacher at Whitefield Supplementary School. It is an honour to be able to set an example to students, staff and parents and to promote education. The skills I have gained include leadership skills, communication skills with people at all levels, time management, meeting deadlines, team work and decision-making. I have consistently shown myself to be reliable, honest, trustworthy and responsible.

I am constantly learning and this summer I will attend a one-day RSC conference organized by and for young chemistry professionals and researchers. I am also proud that I was able to come from Afghanistan and integrate into the UK so quickly and successfully. Although I initially found the language difficult, I excelled in my GCSEs and A-levels and have so far excelled at university.

In 2011, my family and I had some traumatic issues to deal with in Afghanistan. During my second year, this prevented me from achieving top grades. However, I have a track record of bouncing back from adversity and I am committed to continuing my run of first-class results.

I feel that I would be a great asset to any chemistry department. I feel that working in the best research facilities in the world, with gifted chemists, will enable me to thrive. Being among the best students will be a great privilege and a real opportunity for me to focus on and achieve what I love to do – medicinal chemistry.

Exercise: Spotting the techniques used

What type of introduction has Faheela used?

Overall, why is the first paragraph effective?

Why is the first-person viewpoint effective in a personal statement?

What specific examples does she use in paragraphs 2 and 3 to express her passion for, and interest in, chemistry?

What specific skills and personal attributes does Faheela express in paragraph 4?

How does Faheela relate her past work experience to the course she wishes to study?

Referring back to the seven stories earlier in this chapter, what story does she use in paragraph 8?

How would you describe the tone used throughout the document?

What writing techniques (from Chapter 5) and literary techniques (from Chapter 4) has Faheela used throughout? Give examples.

What type of ending has she used? Why is this effective?

Based on reading the personal statement alone, would you give Faheela a place on the course? Give reasons why.

Exercise: Writing a personal statement

In writing her personal statement, Faheela successfully combined many of the techniques used in this book. So, take inspiration from her document and see how you can weave in your own experience, skills, enthusiasm and goals and hopes for the future by writing your own personal statement. But before you do so, ensure that you can effectively answer the following questions:

- Why do you want to do this course?
- Why have you chosen this particular university?
- What strengths/experience do you have that make the course ideally suited to you?
- Who or what has particularly inspired you?
- Where do you see yourself in three to five years' time?
- How will you reach your ultimate career goals?

Next, decide on a strong introduction and use Faheela's statement as a template for your own.

Tackling other further study documents

Economics graduate Michael had been admitted onto a summer course in Global Energy Dilemmas in preparation for taking a PhD. Along with his fellow students, he was asked to submit a 300-word 'statement of purpose' outlining his reasons for joining the course. As many people would, he kept this very objective and professional and as a result the statement lacked punch and dynamism and revealed little about his personality.

For instance, he began,

> A focus of my graduate study research was the influence of climate policy design on technological change. In my thesis I discussed the theory about how stringent environmental regulations may spur innovation and consequently support the transition to low carbon energies.

I advised Michael to introduce himself in a personal way and to use a more powerful opening to give an insight into his personality. He decided to use the 'story in a snapshot' technique, telling a personal story about how he became interested in the environment and climate change. His revised statement began,

> I first became interested in environmental issues at secondary school. As part of a geography project I made a short documentary film showing illegal rubbish disposal scattered all over town. I was aggravated by the alarming disrespect for nature. From then, I decided to become involved in defending the environment. This interest followed me throughout my studies. At graduate level I specialized in environmental economics, focusing mainly on climate policy design and how it can influence the shift to environment-friendly technology. In my Master's thesis I chose to write about 'the Porter hypothesis'. The model encourages exceptionally stringent environmental regulations as a way to spur innovation. Porter argues that provoking innovation efforts supports the transition to low carbon technologies, without causing any profit loss – creating a 'win–win' solution.

This version is much more effective and presents Michael as a dynamic, focused individual with excellent academic credentials.

Job hunting documents

The golden rules for job applications are that you must use the audience tracker technique and you must be specific. Remember that the employer has carefully designed a job and is now looking for someone who fits it exactly. So, you need to study a job advert and understand the words it uses in the same way that you analysed essay questions. The previous exercise and writing your personal stories can help you write about your personal qualities in a compelling way. This is because you also have to understand what your readers' objections might be and address them.

Writing CVs

I'm not going to provide a CV template as there are many available through Microsoft Office and countless other internet resources. Instead, this section will focus on the writing skills you need once you get down to the nitty-gritty of preparing the content.

- Make sure that your CV is full of action words. These are verbs such as 'created', 'delivered', 'trained', 'mentored', 'planned', 'worked', 'promoted', 'helped', 'assisted', 'sold', 'arranged', 'developed', 'generated', 'conducted', 'undertook', 'located', 'managed', 'achieved' and 'devised'. These words instantly make the content more punchy and dynamic. So, instead of writing 'Promotion of organization's events (email, flyers)' write 'Promoted organization's events through creating and distributing emails and flyers.'
- Leave yourself out of it, so remove the word 'I' and just state what you did in the third person. You can do this by simply putting the verb at the beginning of the sentence (see above). And ensure that you write about three different responsibilities for each job or position you present. These should relate to the skills that the employers have said they are looking for.
- If you're still at university, about to graduate or are a recent graduate, put your education at the top. If not, leave it until the end.
- Be specific in describing what you did, using numbers where possible. So, if you worked as an editor for your student newspaper, for instance, don't just say that you managed a team of writers – say how many.
- Tailor your CV to the purpose for which it was intended so that the readers can get a sense that you're perfectly suited to the opportunity at hand.
- Highlight the skills you've gained that are transferable. Keep in mind the soft skills outlined at the beginning of this chapter that employers are looking for. For example, even if all you've done is hand out flyers for a local rock band, make sure you use language that shows you are reliable, hardworking and have the confidence to approach members of the public.
- If you feel your CV doesn't make logical sense (in that it doesn't explain your path from one subject or job to another) then take the back to front approach. Start from your current goal and then explain your work and education history in terms of it. So if you've studied French and Politics but

now decide you want a job in marketing, then explain the experiences and skills you've developed on the way and how they can help in a marketing career. For instance, French translation requires patience, diligence and accuracy, things also needed when dealing with marketing campaigns.

- Finally, the quality of the writing in your CV has a lot to do with the quality of both your thinking and the subsequent editing once you have all your thoughts on paper. Be ruthless in weeding out extra words and make your writing as tight and focused as possible. But be sure to write in full sentences.

Modelling an effective cover letter

The purpose of a cover letter is to get you a job interview, so in essence you have to construct it as a powerful piece of persuasive writing. A good cover letter can stand the test of time. You can use it again and again throughout your career, simply adapting it depending on which position you're applying for and including the new skills and experience you've gained. So, it's worth spending considerable time on it and ensuring that it's as excellent as possible.

Here's an example of a winning cover letter from my student Gail that enabled her to land her chosen role. Notice that she has a powerful opening and ending and has made every word count. I have removed the names of people, organizations and her university in the cover letter.

> Dear *[name of recruiter]*
>
> I am passionate about digital work and having seen your job advert for a Social Media Assistant I felt I had to apply. I am eager to bring value to *[insert name of organisation]* and feel that I have much to offer.
>
> I recently graduated in Environmental Sciences from one of the best UK universities *[insert name of university]* and I am an 'all-rounder'. I have two years' experience in communications using social media and content management systems (Typo3, Word Press). During that time I have launched two websites *[insert names of sites]*. With my communication skills, I am the link between programmers and the superiors at the companies I have interned at. Since I arrived in London six months ago, I managed to build up a network and have some freelance clients already. I create websites for them, consult with them on social media strategies according to their needs and implement social media tools for them, when needed. For example, I manage several accounts and still communicate for them on different social media platforms such as Twitter, Facebook, Google Plus, Pinterest, YouTube and LinkedIn.

I work in an efficient and structured manner, independently as well as in teams. Thanks to my broad background in environmental studies, I adapt quickly to new work settings. I speak and write French, German and English fluently. I may lack additional experience in design but I am eager and willing to learn. Also, I am happy to travel for my work and would be available immediately. Lastly, I am convinced that my dedication and know-how can support *[name of organisation]* and its clients effectively in fulfilling its goals to deliver globally from early phase to completion.

I hope, having read the above and my CV that you will consider me for the role of Social Media Assistant. I look forward to meeting you to discuss my skills in more detail and to see how they could fit your needs. In the meantime, if you should have any questions, please call me on *[phone number]*

Yours sincerely

Gail Finley

Exercise: Writing a cover letter

Just as with personal statements, there are many questions you need to ask yourself before writing one. Answer the questions below and your answers will form the structure of your cover letter.

- Why you are applying for the role? Explain this in one or two sentences.
- In what ways are you ideal for the role?
- What specific/relevant tasks have you done in previous jobs or in your studies?
- How do these relate to the role you're applying for?
- What are you currently doing?
- What general skills have you developed through education and work?
- How are these directly related to the role you're applying for?
- What objections could the employer have that might prevent them from hiring you? How can you address these?
- What is the winning statement that you hope will make them employ you?

Prepare a finished cover letter that you feel best represents your skills and abilities, and remember that unless you are applying for a range of very similar jobs, you will need to tailor it to suit each individual position.

The dos and don'ts of job applications

- Don't write 'Dear Sir/Madam'. The recruiter will think you lack the initiative even to find out if they are male or female. If the name of the person isn't listed in the advert, call or go on the internet to find it out.
- Remember to use the spell checker – even minor spelling mistakes can mean your application is discarded.
- Don't ever put yourself down in an application – highlight your strengths and address your weaknesses by either turning them into a positive or saying you are willing to learn. For example, you could write, 'I may not have much experience but I am enthusiastic, willing to go the extra mile and will do everything it takes to learn fully about the industry.'
- If you need to fill in an application form rather than send a CV, don't do it off the cuff. Select sections from your CV and thoughtfully craft additional sentences and sections using the techniques learnt in this chapter.

Turning academic writing into business writing

The golden rule in business writing (or workplace writing) is: less is more. Good business writing is plain, simple and straightforward. At university, you get marks for being ambivalent, not committing to a point of view, being impartial and heavily referencing the work of others. But in business writing, you need to be bold, straightforward and direct and have a point of view. You can also state what others think, but what *you* think is most important. So when it comes to writing letters, memos, emails, reports and other business documents, you'll have to leave behind many of the things that have stood you in great stead so far in your student life.

The main comment I've heard from my students is that they are afraid to be direct and straightforward in their writing and use of language at work – they think that it's inappropriate and perhaps even rude! They have already learnt so many rules at school that they are terrified of breaking them.

However, if you've worked hard at mastering the techniques in this book then you already have the skills necessary to produce good business writing. Whatever you write at work, you need to ensure that it:

- is targeted to the readers – and tells them what to do after receiving the document;
- has a powerful introduction and conclusion – including a 'call to action', if necessary;
- has attention-grabbing titles and subtitles;

- uses the active voice and verbs instead of nouns;
- uses short sentences – approximately 20–25 words per sentence;
- uses direct language – words such as 'I', 'you', 'we', 'us', 'our' and 'your';
- uses simple words – avoiding too much jargon or abbreviations.

If you choose to work in an office-based environment, you'll spend a considerable amount of your time writing emails, reports and other documents. However, a study by the Association of Graduate Recruiters found that 56 per cent of employers surveyed said they were concerned by graduates' poor reading and writing skills (BBC 2008). Employers are increasingly recognizing the economic value of good writing. If you can impress employers with your writing skills, you'll be well ahead of the competition.

Further reading

Grappo, G. J. ([1994] 1997) *Get the Job You Want in 30 Days*. Berkley Books.

Student Comment

Ben, IT graduate

'I have done work experience in some companies and at first I was intimidated by the types of writing that my colleagues produced. I honestly thought that complicated writing showed that you were more professional, intelligent and successful. But now I see that it's not effective because it doesn't allow the writers and readers to communicate properly. Now I understand that the secret is to substitute plain, simple words for complicated, academic words.'

Greta says:

'In Chapter 5, we looked at the formal, academic words that you needed to learn from your degree. Depending on your job, it's likely that you'll have to unlearn these to write in a plain simple way. To help you with this, visit www.plainenglish.co.uk/free-guides to download your free, personal copy of the A–Z of alternative words which will help you to choose simple versions of complicated words.'

Part V

Finishing touches

Chapter 13

A complete writing checklist

This chapter consists of an extensive checklist, where you can mark off the techniques you have learnt and ensure that you are using them – where appropriate – in your written work. Not every technique you've learnt is listed here. Instead, these are the main ones that you need to use during the writing process. The techniques in italics are best reserved for more informal documents. Later, there are some actual examples of common errors from essays to help you improve.

Reading techniques

Active reading checklist	❑
Literary techniques checklist	❑

Creative tools and techniques

Object writing	❑
Metaphor table (to create metaphors and similes)	❑
Alliteration	❑
Personification	❑
Symbolism	❑

Irony ❑

Sibilance ❑

Onomatopoeia ❑

Repetition ❑

Writing skills techniques

Writing introductions

Story in a snapshot ❑

The element of surprise ❑

A blast from the past ❑

The way it is ❑

From the horse's mouth ❑

Reporting the news ❑

Writing conclusions

Round-up, round-up ❑

Crystal ball gazing ❑

From the horse's mouth (in summary) ❑

All-purpose writing skills techniques

Audience tracker ❑

Just one sentence ❑

Active voice (with occasional use of the passive voice) ❑

Verbs instead of nouns ❑

- Keep it simple ❑
- Being specific ❑
- Short sentences and phrases ❑
- Pick 'n' mix linking words ❑
- Rewriting, editing and proofreading ❑
- Checking strategy ❑

Formal writing skills

- Formal words and phrases ❑
- Formal linking words ❑
- Third-person viewpoint ❑
- Effective use of evidence ❑

Informal writing skills

- Informal words and phrases ❑
- Plays on words ❑
- First-person, second-person and imperative viewpoints ❑
- Informal linking words ❑
- The power of three ❑

Common essay errors

Here are some examples from degree students' essays, where their technique has gone awry.

Unnecessary use of the passive voice

The following passage uses the passive voice: 'The Board of Estimate's request to influence the department's budget to $2.64 million was granted by the jury.' To make it active, it should read: 'The jury granted the Board of Estimate's . . .'

Ineffective use of evidence and evaluation

Here the student overstates the meaning of the data: 'Such a rise in population will have a dramatic consequence for the level of poverty in sub-Saharan Africa.' You must be able to back up statements so it's better to put the word 'may' rather than 'will' if there's no proof that something will definitely happen.

Being too general

Here, the student needs to be more specific about how many people hold misconceptions. Instead of writing: 'Many students hold misconceptions about science and they do not know their ideas are incorrect', she could write 'Studies have shown that virtually all students hold misconceptions . . .'

Lack of explanation

The following sentence assumes that the reader knows all about the people mentioned: 'This chapter explores how the restrictions on theatre have impacted playwrights such as Wu Han and actors such as Xiao Cuihus.' The student needs to explain who Han and Cuihus are.

Unnecessary repetition

This section was written as part of an essay explaining why in some parts of the developing world, families prefer to have male children. 'Most families prefer to have boys as they are cheaper. This is because culture and tradition dictates that a girl's parents have to pay the groom's family a dowry when she marries. Therefore, girls are often seen as an expense that families can ill afford. And it is because of the expenses related to marriage that most families prefer to have male children.' The last sentence is redundant and can be deleted as it simply repeats information that the writer has already given. Don't include this type of repetition throughout essays as you can eat up words unnecessarily and then not have space to include valuable content.

Failure to proofread

Sometimes, it's easy to include typos in the most unlikely places, such as in titles and headings, as in 'Britain' and 'Wimbledon' in this article: 'Manolo Santana says Britian won't win Wimdledon – and shouldn't count on Murray'.

Overusing jargon

While it's important to include key words, don't go overboard. Take the following example: 'Fast food outlets, vending machines, not having enough cycle lanes or healthy transport options are micro and macro elements that contribute to an area becoming an obesogenic environment.' Micro and macro are commonly used academic terms, but obesogenic veers into jargon territory and could be written in a simpler way.

References

Adey, P. and Shayer, M. (1993) An exploration of long-term far-transfer effects following an extended intervention programme in the high school science curriculum, *Cognition and Instruction*, 11(1): 1–29.

Ardington, A. (2011) Writing: an essential and powerful communication tool for today's 'three dimensional' engineering graduate, *Journal of Academic Writing*, 1 (Autumn): 62–3.

Bartleby.com (1989) *Inaugural Addresses of the Presidents of the United States*. Available at http://www.bartleby.com/124/pres61.html [Accessed 15 August 2012].

BBC (2008) Graduate literacy 'worries firms'. Available at http://news.bbc.co.uk/2/hi/uk_news/education/7494172.stm [Accessed 15 August 2012].

Bloomberg Businessweek (2010) *From Russia with Gloves*, 1 July. Available at http://www.businessweek.com/magazine/content/10_28/b4186069472284.htm [Accessed 15 August 2012].

Booker, C. (2005) *The Seven Basic Plots: Why We Tell Stories*. New York/London: Continuum International Publishing Group Ltd.

Campbell, J. ([1949] 2008) *The Hero with a Thousand Faces*, 3rd edition. Novato, CA: New World Library.

Dominican University (2008) Dominican University of California study backs up strategies for achieving goals. Available at http://www.dominican.edu/dominicannews/study-backs-up-strategies-for-achieving-goals [Accessed 15 August 2012].

Epstein, S. (1998) *Constructive Thinking: The Key to Emotional Intelligence*. San Francisco, CA: Greenwood Press.

Ganobcsik-Williams, L. (2004) *A Report on the Teaching of Academic Writing in UK Higher Education*. Available at http://www.rlf.org.uk/fellowshipscheme/research.cfm [Accessed 18 August 2012].

Gazzaniga, M. S. (2005) Forty-five years of split-brain research and still going strong, *Nature Reviews Neuroscience*, 6: 653–9.

Geda, Y., Roberts, L. K., Roberts, R., Pankratz, V., Christianson, T., Mielke, M. *et al.* (2012) Caloric intake, aging, and mild cognitive impairment: a population-based study, *American Academy of Neurology*. Available at www.aan.com/globals/axon/assets/9279.pdf [Accessed 18 August 2012].

Goleman, D. (1995) *Emotional Intelligence*. New York: Bantam Books.

Human Genetics Commission (2009) HGC statement on genetic testing and personalised nutrition. Available from http://www.hgc.gov.uk/Client/Content.asp?Contentld=846 [Accessed 25 September 2011].

Hume, D. (1758) *Squashed Philosophers: David Hume Enquiry Concerning Human Understanding*. Available at http://www.btinternet.com/~glynhughes/squashed/hume.htm [Accessed 15 August 2012].

Lally, P. *et al.* (2010) How are habits formed? Modelling habit formation in the real world, *European Journal of Social Psychology*, 40 (6): 998–1009.

McMillan, I. (2010) We need to reduce our noise footprint. Available at http://www.guardian.co.uk/commentisfree/2010/sep/12/noise-footprint-ipod-motorbike [Accessed 17 August 2012].

Maltz, M. (1960) *Psycho-Cybernetics*. London: Prentice-Hall.

MBTI Basics (2012) Available at http://www.myersbriggs.org/my-mbti-personality-type/mbti-basics/ [Accessed 15 August 2012].

NHS (2012) *Smoking, Drinking and Drug Use among Young People in England in 2011*. Available at http://www.ic.nhs.uk/pubs/sdd11fullreport [Accessed 19 August 2012].

Office for National Statistics, *Graduates in the Labour Market – 2012*. Available at http://www.ons.gov.uk/ons/rel/lmac/graduates-in-the-labour-market/2012/graduates-in-the-labour-market.html [Accessed 15 August 2012].

Orel, P. (2006) Music helps students retain math. Available at http://urwebsrv.rutgers.edu/focus/article/link/1779/ [Accessed 15 August 2012].

Paré, A. and Smart, G. (1994) Observing genres in action: towards a research methodology, in A. Freeman and P. Medway (eds) *Genre and the New Rhetoric*, pp.146–54. London: Taylor and Francis.

Pattison, P. (1995) *Writing Better Lyrics*. Cincinnati, OH: Writer's Digest Books.

Pennebaker, J. W. and Chung, C. K. (2007) Expressive writing, emotional upheavals, and health, in H. Friedman and R. Silver (eds) *Handbook of Health Psychology*, pp. 263–84. New York: Oxford University Press.

SMITH (2012) *Everyone has a story. What's yours?* Available at http://www.smithmag.net/ [Accessed 15 August 2012].

Tharp, T. (2007) *The Creative Habit: Learn It and Use It for Life*. New York: Simon & Schuster.

Westwood, S., Pritchard, A. and Morgan, N.J. (2000) Gender-blind marketing: businesswomen's perceptions of airline services, *Tourism Management*, 21(4): 353–62.

Wheeler, V. (2007) Much ado about a muffin at BA, *Sun*, 19 December. Available at http://www.thesun.co.uk/sol/homepage/news/599226/British-Airways-Suspends-steward-Eating-a-muffin.html [Accessed 15 August 2012].

WSH Council (2008) *Workplace Safety & Health 2008 (January–June) National Statistics*. Available from https://www.wshc.sg/wps/PA_InfoStop/download?folder=IS2010012500098&file=MOM_Statistical_report_2008%20(Full%20Report).pdf [Accessed 15 August 2012].

Index

Locators shown in *italics* refer to tables, questionnaires, exercises and worksheets.

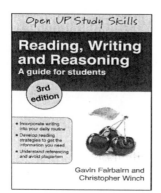